So, Tell Me a Story

So, Tell Me a Story

The Art of Storytelling
for Teaching and Preaching

Stephen Farris

CASCADE *Books* · Eugene, Oregon

SO, TELL ME A STORY
The Art of Storytelling for Teaching and Preaching

Cascade Books
An Imprint of Wipf and Stock Publishers
199 W. 8th Ave., Suite 3
Eugene, OR 97401

www.wipfandstock.com

PAPERBACK ISBN: 978-1-5326-3749-0
HARDCOVER ISBN: 978-1-5326-3750-6
EBOOK ISBN: 978-1-5326-3751-3

Cataloging-in-Publication data:

Names: Farris, Stephen, author.

Title: So, tell me a story : the art of storytelling for teaching and preaching / Stephen Farris.

Description: Eugene, OR: Cascade Books. | Includes bibliographical references.

Identifiers: ISBN: 978-1-5326-3749-0 (paperback). | ISBN: 978-1-5326-3750-6 (hardcover). | ISBN: 978-1-5326-3751-3 (epub).

Subjects: LCSH: Preaching. | Storytelling—Religious aspects—Christianity. | Narrative theology.

Classification: BV4211.3 F37 2018 (print) | BV4211.3 (ebook).

Manufactured in the U.S.A.   JULY 17, 2018

Contents

Acknowledgments

I owe thanks beyond words to many people. Perhaps I ought to mention first the many churches and other groups on whom I have tried out the material in this book. If I listed all those who have listened to my stories with patience beyond my deserving, the acknowledgements would threaten to become longer than the book. But I must certainly mention in this connection two churches in which I have preached regularly in the recent past, Kerrisdale Presbyterian Church, Vancouver, BC, and Grace Presbyterian Church, Calgary. The material was first set out in a (semi) organized fashion for a workshop for the Synod of Alberta of the Presbyterian Church in Canada and subsequently in a course, "The Art of Storytelling" for Vancouver School of Theology. The course was memorable both for the fact that it was my last before formal retirement and because of the quality of the students.

I am grateful to the Board of St. Andrew's Hall, Vancouver, where I had the privilege of serving as Dean for a dozen years. My time in that position would be a baker's dozen years if one includes a sabbatical leave granted by the Board, during which I wrote the final draft of most of this book. I wish to express my thanks particularly to David Jennings, convener of the Board in the period during which this book was written, a friend as well as a superlative Board convener. The relationship between St. Andrew's Hall and Vancouver School of Theology is too complex to lay out here, but I cannot thank the Board of St. Andrew's Hall without also expressing my gratitude to the Board and Faculty of Vancouver School of Theology, especially to Principal Richard Topping. In connection with this sabbatical leave, I must also mention the residents of the village of Aniane in Languedoc, France. The odds of anyone from the village ever reading these words are very small indeed, but it is only right to say *merci* for their courtesy and their patience with my attempts to speak their beautiful language. There are some stories in that connection . . .

I must also thank the staff of Cascade Books, who have made the production of this book possible. My gratitude goes to K. C. Hanson, James Stock, Matthew Wimer, Jeremy Funk, and Heather Carraher. In one respect the work of the publisher's staff was materially lessened. My daughter-in-law, Judith, a very skilled writer herself, edited the manuscript in detail. This is surely a task that cannot be found in the official daughter-in-law's job description! Thank you for this work, and, even more, for caring for Allan and the grandchildren.

In the end, however, my thanks must go primarily not only to those who serve as the listeners to my stories but to those who form the essence of my story. I always give thanks first for my wife, Patty, whose constant love and support gives joy to my story. What I feel about her is beyond my words. I remember with thanksgiving my late father, the Reverend Professor Allan Farris, who told some of the stories in the book, and my mother, Muriel Farris, now also at rest. Among the many gifts of love she gave were countless sessions reading aloud to her children. That is surely the best way to learn to love words and love stories. The word that she was dying came to us in France the night of the Paris terrorist attacks, but despite the travel complexities caused by those despicable acts we arrived home in time for me to hold her hand while she passed to her Lord. I could not wish her back with us, given what she suffered, but I do wish that she could have known of the publication of this book.

I told stories to and sometimes borrowed stories from my own sons, Allan and Daniel. For them and for their loving wives, Judith and Gillian, I give thanks. But I hope that my storytelling days are not merely a remembrance of things past but also an activity of the future. So I give thanks for my grandchildren, for Anna, Peter, Idris, and any others yet to come. To them I dedicate this book with the warning that their Opa, who loves them very much, will inflict stories on them as long as he is able.

Some of the stories in or behind this book were first told me by my father when as a ten year old boy I walked with him through the streets of Geneva. He translated for me the Latin of the motto of the Genevan Reformation, *Soli Deo Gloria*. I remember those words and close with them: To God alone be the glory!

Introduction

Why People Invited Jesus to Dinner

Anyone who reads the Gospels will catch on very quickly that Jesus had enemies. The Gospels specify some of the accusations of those enemies. This is one, according to both Luke and Matthew: "the Son of Man has come eating and drinking, and you say, 'Look, a glutton and a drunkard, a friend of tax collectors and sinners!'" (Luke 7:34; cf. Matt 11:19). A contemporary translation might be, "You call me a party animal."

Particularly in the story according to the Gospel of Luke, it could be claimed that there are grounds for this accusation. Jesus is constantly being invited out to dinner; he probably enjoys the food and wine, and he certainly is a friend of tax collectors and sinners. Before he had enemies, however, he had hosts. There are many good and edifying ways of explaining all this, suitable to the seriousness of the typical sermon. In the presence of Jesus, people of all sorts, especially those whom the community called sinners, became aware of their deepest spiritual needs. By sharing table fellowship with them, Jesus declared that they were accepted by God, and whatever their past they were once again children of Abraham and of a loving Abba. All that is true. But perhaps this simpler statement is also true: people enjoyed Jesus's company. They liked being with him and therefore invited him to dinner, and apparently all those lumpish disciples along with him. Now, this is only a guess, but it rings true to me. They liked being with Jesus, at least at the beginning, and so they invited him to dinner . . . and perhaps they liked being with Jesus because he told such good stories.

SO, TELL US A STORY

I came by an interest in stories and storytelling honestly. My late father, Allan Leonard Farris, told stories too, most often at the dinner table, but also in the living room, on the deck, while driving the car (sometimes when he ought to have been paying full attention to the road), or in just about any other circumstance. Funny stories elicited loud laughter, serious stories brought sudden stillness, sad stories left listeners with moistened eyes: the stories were of every type. Dad was a Presbyterian minister and a professor of church history. That may sound grim, but actually he was one of those historians who have never forgotten that at the root of the word and the discipline of history is that simple word *story*, so listening to him tell his tales was fun, even the ones about church history. We had the usual father-son tensions in other ways, but the stories were almost always enjoyable. So, as I say, I grew up listening to my Dad tell stories, many of them repeatedly. If a story is worth telling once, it's usually worth telling again . . . and again.

When my dad wasn't telling stories himself, his friends were responding in kind, passing on their own tales. Many of their stories were also funny, and our house would ring with laughter, but others were more serious and tinged with sadness. Some were even tragic. It didn't matter; most of them were worth hearing. My mom didn't tell stories; she just made sure my brother, sister, and I knew we were loved, and that was more than enough. It is more important to children that they are loved than that they hear stories, though in many cases, including that of my father, telling stories to children is a way of showing love.

It is a wonderful thing to hear a fund of stories from childhood forward. Our imaginations are both awakened and shaped by those stories. It is vital in a Christian upbringing that those stories include, and include very prominently, the stories of Scripture. That was certainly the case with me. But it is an excellent thing also if that fund of stories includes tales from literature and stories drawn from family tradition. (Indeed, what is family tradition but a collection of practices and of stories passed down from one family member to the next?) It is also wonderful if that fund of stories is constantly refreshed by tales of interesting things that we have seen or heard. We are what we are because we are loved (or not loved) and because of the stories we hear. The acorn did not fall far from the tree, and I'm a preacher, a professor, and a storyteller too. To be honest, I tell a lot of the stories over and over again too. Ask my wife or my sons. But you are a new audience, so here are some of my favorites and a few thoughts that spring from them.

Let me clear about this book: it is neither an exposition of narrative theology nor (and this is slightly different) a theology of narrative. Many learned books and essays on exactly those subjects can be found elsewhere. Some theology, some of it even about the theological subject of narrative, will emerge in this book, but when it does so, it is most likely to come from the stories themselves. But then, that's one of the main things stories do in the Christian tradition; they generate and convey theology. Theology might even be defined as systematic reflection on the story of Israel, of Jesus, and of the young church. The framework of the Apostles' Creed, for example, is structured around the story of the life, death, resurrection, and return in glory of Jesus Christ. Story sometimes, perhaps often, grows into theology in the Christian tradition. Whatever theology does emerge in this book, directly or indirectly, may not be accidental but will be far from systematic.

Nor is this book intended to be primarily a how-to manual on the skills of storytelling. The first four chapters contain theological reflection on the storyteller's work, together with suggestions and even some practical pointers on the necessary skills and attitudes for effective exercise of the art. These will also emerge chiefly from the stories themselves. There are guides to the skills of storytelling, both inside and outside the church.[1] For the most part, this isn't one of them. I am convinced that the best way to learn to tell stories is to listen to them or to read them, and then to try to tell your own stories yourself.[2] So, mostly, this book is a collection of stories, especially after the first four chapters. And perhaps some wisdom will grow in their telling and hearing.

I am a preacher and a teacher of preaching. When I think of telling stories, I think first of the pulpit, and much of what I write here will apply directly to the work of the preacher. What is said here about the use of stories in preaching will normally apply also to teaching, however. If you are either a preacher or a teacher, you may be able to use some of these

1. See in particular the work of Scott Hoezee, *Actuality*. Other resources may be found in the bibliography of this book.

2. Apparently Saint Augustine agreed. In the first Christian textbook on biblical interpretation and preaching, *De Doctrina Christiana, IV, 3*, he wrote, "For [people] of quick intellect and glowing temperament find it easier to become eloquent by reading and listening to eloquent speakers than by following rules for eloquence." The only question here is why Augustine thought that the observation was true only for those of quick intellect.

stories. You certainly have both my permission and my encouragement to do so. But if you are not a teacher or preacher, or some of the stories don't fit a sermon or a lesson plan, please don't worry about it. Many of these stories have never made it into any of my sermons or lectures, either. This is a conversation; sit down with me at an imaginary table, and share stories. And while the stories go around, perhaps we will reflect a little on Christian life and other such matters. But please don't dismiss the idea that you will never tell stories just because you are not a preacher or teacher. Imagine, for example, that you are a parent of adult children. You could say, "Dear, this is what I think you should do . . ." On the other hand, you might say, "I read an interesting story," and simply let the story sink in. I think this method would work better with my own sons and perhaps that would be the case with your family also. And, if it doesn't work with your children, try the grandchildren!

From time to time, then, we will reflect on the art of storytelling itself. But the stories are the main thing. For the first four chapters of the book, in which the art of storytelling is a significant focus, the stories will appear in italics. The later chapters in the book will largely be collections of stories. Read the stories and skip over the other material, if you like. It is, after all, the stories that matter.

To be more exact, it is *the* story that matters. It is certainly not the case that our stories are the heart of preaching. In my own Reformed tradition, John Calvin didn't tell stories himself and was very hard on those who occupied themselves with storytelling. He speaks very negatively of congregations who long for "pleasing stories and buffoonery or old wives' tales," and of the preachers who give in to that desire.[3] The heart of preaching is an encounter with the living and powerful Word of God who speaks through the written word of the text. A careful engagement with the living Word through the written word is far more important than our winning stories and anecdotes. Sometimes, it must be admitted, telling stories actually gets in the way of that engagement. Telling stories will not replace careful exegesis, theological reflection, and thorough analysis of the contemporary world. We must not go too far here, however. If you are tempted to agree entirely with Calvin that stories have little place in preaching, you might remember a figure who is far more important in

---

3. The excellent standard work on the subject of Calvin's preaching is Parker, *Calvin's Preaching*. My own much smaller contribution to the subject is Farris, "John Calvin and the Preaching of the Lively Word."

the homiletical tradition than Calvin and who was famed for his stories. *"A certain man had two sons and the younger of them said to his father ..."*

Moreover, the Bible is more like a story than anything else. It has been memorably called "one vast, loosely organized, non-fiction novel"[4] and that still remains a sound description of the Scriptures as a whole. Calvin's disdain for stories need not be imitated. There is, in fact, nothing that can or should replace telling the story.

It's Not Over Yet

I remember preaching an anniversary service in a Presbyterian church in a small Ontario town of a little more than two thousand people. The minister was a former student of mine who was enormously helped in his work by the presence in that little church of a man—call him Pete—who had a passionate interest in children and youth, and a gift for reaching out to them. Together they began a youth program that turned out to be amazingly successful. Sometimes they drew as many as seventy-five young people to the program. You will understand from these numbers that these were not all Presbyterians or even kids with any Christian connection whatever. Some of them knew startlingly little about the Christian faith. One of their number was a boy named Marty.

Pete came to the conclusion that some of these young people were completely ignorant of the central stories of our faith. Fortunately, he was a gifted storyteller. As Easter approached, Pete built an imitation campfire in the church basement. (Don't ask me how that was done; I don't know the answer.) Pete dressed up as a shepherd, in a dressing gown and a tea towel bound to the head, to tell the story of Jesus to the group. As Pete told the old, old story, Marty and the rest of the young people followed Jesus to Jerusalem in their imaginations. They watched him heal the sick and give sight to the blind. They listened as the rulers plotted to destroy him and heard the tinkle of thirty pieces of silver, the purchase price of loyalty. They sat with Jesus at table in an upper room and followed him to a garden where he was betrayed by his friend, with a kiss. (Young people do understand the reality of betrayal by a friend.) With each passing episode Marty became more visibly distressed. The young people witnessed the trial, heard Peter deny Jesus and felt the lash of the Roman scourge. They stood by the foot of the cross and in deepest silence watched him die. Marty was transfixed. When Jesus, betrayed

---

4. Kelsey, *Uses of Scripture in Recent Theology*, 45. Kelsey attributes this understanding to Karl Barth.

and abandoned, drew his last shuddering breath, Marty could take it no more. He cried out in sorrow, "Oh, mannn!"

A young person from the church, someone who knew the story, laid his hand on Marty's arm and said, "That's all right Marty. It's not over yet."

That's the Christian story. In a world of sorrow, pain, and ultimately death, "It's not over yet."

Sometimes amazing things can happen when we tell the story, or even a story that orients our minds in the direction of the story.

1

What Stories Do

WHAT IS A STORY?

Perhaps a short working definition of *story* would be helpful.[1] *A story is the intersection of plot and character.* In this definition, I am following literary critic of the Gospels Stephen D. Moore: "Being preoccupied with story means, most of all, being preoccupied with *plot* and *character* . . . Plot and character are inseparably bound up in the reading experience . . . Each works to produce the other. Characters are defined in and through the plot, by what they do and what they say. The plot in turn comes into view as characters act and interact. Characters are further defined by what the narrator and fellow characters say about them.[2]"

Stories may be contrasted with what may be called observations, for want of a better term. The dividing line between a story and an observation is fuzzy but recognizable. This is clearly an observation:

It always seems to me that it is harder to forgive others for being right than being wrong.

---

1. Note that it would be possible to allow the working definition of *story* to emerge from the telling of the stories themselves. Perhaps it would have been more methodologically consistent to do so. But then, storytellers worry less about methodological consistency than do systematicians.

2. Moore, *Literary Criticism and the Gospels* 14, 15.

This is an observation that seems widely true, but no particular examples of the difficulty are supplied by the speaker in this case. Observations can be very valuable, particularly if they are more concrete than this one, appealing also to the senses. There is a whole book of such observations in the Bible, namely, the book of Proverbs. An observation begins to resemble a story when something happens and the speaker begins to describe a specific instance of what he or she has seen generally.

Have you ever watched spiders weave their webs in some difficult corner? They often fail, but they keep on trying.

One might even add the familiar phrase "If at first you don't succeed, try, try again." That is very close to a rudimentary story. But there can be no mistake about what this is:

The Spider

Long, long ago, hundreds of years ago, there lived a man in Scotland named Robert the Bruce. Robert the Bruce laid claim to the throne of Scotland as its king. In his time, however, the King of England sent a great army to invade Scotland and to seize it for his own. Robert the Bruce gathered a ragtag army of brave Scots to fight the English, but they were defeated. Six times, he gathered his men, and six times they were defeated by the English.

The last battle was so terrible a defeat that Robert the Bruce and his remaining men had to scatter and hide in the wilderness. Robert the Bruce himself took refuge in a cave. Tired, sad, defeated, and alone he sat by a meager fire. By the light of the fire, he saw a spider begin to weave her web by hanging a strand from the ceiling of the cave. It failed. But the spider tried again . . . and failed. Six times the spider tried and failed. "Something else knows what it is to fail six times," thought Robert the Bruce. But the spider tried again, a seventh time. This time the strand held. And soon a magnificent web spread through the corner of the cave.

Robert the Bruce took heart, gathered his men yet again, and this time he succeeded. The Scots won a great victory. The English left their land, the Scots were free, and Robert the Bruce was their king.

If at first you don't succeed, try, try again.

If you doubt the story, the Scots will show you the cave; in fact, they will show you several caves where the spider weaved her web! Actually the story was first told, so far as we know, five centuries after the life of Robert the Bruce, by the Scottish novelist Sir Walter Scott, and it is more moral instruction than history. That does not matter for the purposes of this book, however. The observation has become a story, an often told story, familiar especially to those of Scottish descent. The distinction between that observation and the story lies in this matter of plot and character. Stories, in order to be stories rather than observations, must have at least one character who engages in action or reflection, and something must happen in or to that person; or to say the same thing in short form, stories must have plot and character. Observations, which may lack one or other or both characteristics, are also useful in preaching and teaching, but that would take us into a different book. Or as storytellers sometimes say, "But that would be another story." This book is about stories.

Given the length of the stories that appear in preaching and teaching, we are not talking *War and Peace* when it comes to complication of plot or cast of characters. One may think of Jesus's parables here: not all the parables are stories. Some may be more rightly described as extended metaphors.[3] But if we think of the most familiar and best-loved parables, for example, the so-called Prodigal Son or the Good Samaritan, we do see an intersection of plot and character. Something happens in or to the characters. The characters are few and the plot is simple, but both are there. These are stories rather than observations or extended metaphors. But even the lengthier parables are relatively short. So it will often be with the stories we tell in preaching and teaching.

By the way, something I have put in these introductory materials that stories usually don't have: footnotes. One time, after listening to an overdeveloped and too-carefully qualified student sermon of mine, my father gently told me, "Son, you can't footnote a sermon." True, and you probably should not footnote a story either.

WHAT STORIES DO

The great Christian theologian and proponent of rhetoric Augustine of Hippo wrote the first textbook on scriptural Interpretation and preaching,

---

3. Scholars of parables have tended to treat all of the gospel parables as one genre. Maybe they are not. Perhaps some are stories and some are extended metaphors.

De Doctrina Christiana, or in English, *On Christian Doctrine.* There he wrote, "Accordingly, a great orator has truly said that an eloquent man must speak so as to teach, delight, and persuade."[4] The "great orator" was Roman lawyer and philosopher Cicero, famed for his eloquence. Augustine is not quite accurately quoting Cicero. But the slight misquotation is actually more useful for our purposes than the original. Let me imitate Augustine and also quote my source not quite accurately: I'll change the order of the elements slightly to say that just as in rhetoric, so in storytelling for preaching and teaching, three essential aims are to delight, to teach, and to persuade.

I will be using some of the categories of classical rhetoric, not because I am an expert on the subject, but because I think they are simple and understandable, yet profound. They can help us understand what we are doing when we are telling stories.[5] But to return to the stories themselves, often stories carry out more than one of these functions; it's not always easy to assign a single function—to delight, to teach, or to persuade—to a given story. Here is a story that fulfills the first function, however:

Stories Delight

The Luckiest Man in Canada

A number of years ago, when veterans of World War II were still both numerous and vigorous, I knew a man named Ed, himself a veteran. One day in the coffee hour after church, he said to me, "Stephen, I think I'm the luckiest man in Canada."

"Oh, why is that, Ed?" I asked. In response, he told me, that he had joined the Canadian Army during World War II and was posted to England. While there, he developed a severe and incurable bacterial abscess on the spine. He was told that the abscess would inevitably grow until it snapped his spine and killed him. Tragically, nothing could be done about it. The army

---

4. Augustine, *On Christian Doctrine* 4.2.27.

5. A standard textbook on classical rhetoric is Corbett and Connors, *Classical Rhetoric for the Modern Student.* The work is both thorough and accessible. It is also expensive and might be better consulted in a library rather than purchased. With respect to the matters raised in this chapter, the 3rd ed. (1990) would do just as well. It can be purchased far more cheaply.

then invalided him back to his home in Winnipeg, Manitoba, to await the eventual outcome in a military hospital.

Ed said he didn't feel particularly ill at that point. He even managed to take a couple of courses in engineering, which would later become his life work. But he knew what was coming. Then one day he was called into the office of the medical doctor in charge of the hospital. The doctor said, "They've sent a new medicine over from England. There are only three samples in the country, one in Montreal, another in Vancouver, and one here. We don't know what it will do. I thought we might test it on you since, frankly, it can't possibly do any harm to a man who's going to die anyways. Would you be willing to give it a try for us?"

Ed thought for a minute, realized he had nothing to lose, and agreed.

The doctor said, "It has to be injected into the buttocks. Pull down your trousers and bend over." Ed complied. It was an order, after all!

A beautiful blonde nurse came into the office with a needle that in Ed's memory was approximately the size of a horse syringe and injected the experimental medicine. You've probably guessed what it was by now. After all, Ed was still around to tell me the story. It was one of the very first batches of penicillin ever used in North America. In those early days it worked like magic on bacteria that had not yet grown drug resistant, and Ed was totally cured. "That's amazing!" I said. "You really are the luckiest man in Canada!"

Ed nodded and added, "That's not all . . . I married the nurse!"

And he looked across the room to his wife, still beautiful after fifty years.

Then he repeated, "I am the luckiest man in Canada."

I've never figured out how to work that story into a sermon or class, other than as an example of a story that delights. Perhaps it could be used in a sermon or lesson on the concepts of luck and blessing. Like most people in the church, however, I have never quite worked out the relationship between those two. It's enough to say that Ed was blessed in several ways. But it doesn't matter that I have never worked out an edifying use for the story. Stories are worth telling for their own sake even if they make no edifying point. It is often sufficient that they delight. Never underestimate the value of delight. It is first, not necessarily in importance, but because the delight we experience in hearing a good story will often open the way for teaching or for persuasion. Even if that does not happen, however, delight is in itself a good thing. It is, after all, a faint but genuine echo of the delight that God takes in a good creation.

In our society, the category delight might almost be replaced by the word *amuse*. It is possible that the kind of story most frequently told in Western society is the joke. This may be true, but it would be a sad limitation of the richness of the category to narrow delight to amusement, or to consider the main function of a story to be the provoking of laughter. It is true that listeners to the "Luckiest Man in Canada" story usually do laugh heartily at the line "I married the nurse." I am convinced, however, that this story is something more than a joke. For one thing, in jokes we often laugh at someone or something, and the ultimate basis of the joke is often pain, even if the pain is as trivial as treading on a slippery banana peel. Here we laugh with Ed at the way the sheer goodness of life sometimes breaks in even in the midst of the most peculiar and even painful circumstances. If we attribute that in-breaking of the goodness of life to God, perhaps we have made a theological statement after all.

Stories Teach

The Casserole

Luke 10:38-42

Stories also teach in a variety of ways. This is one of the stories Dad told me late in his life, and he didn't laugh when he passed it on to me. In fact, his eyes were distinctly moist, if I remember correctly. There may be delight in the story, especially in the coda, but it also teaches.

My father was ordained and began his ministry in First Presbyterian Church in Trail, British Columbia, in the war-wearied but hopeful spring of 1945. Given the congregation and the community, the name First Presbyterian was surely a sign of wild optimism. (Even Presbyterians can be optimists!) It's very hard to imagine that there will ever be a Second Presbyterian Church in that town. Trail is located in the Kootenay Mountains of British Columbia, on the banks of the Columbia River, just before it flows into Washington State. The Kootenays in that region are not spectacular crags and castles of stone like the Rockies or the Cascades. They are steep, jumbled, and covered with forest—but not near Trail. In those days the pollution had all but stripped the hills bare of vegetation, something which, I'm glad to say, is no longer true. At that time Trail was the worst point source of pollution in North America, all because of the giant smelter that is to this very day the town's main employer. I wouldn't be at all surprised if the pollution were the root cause of the saddest part of this story.

First Church was probably healthier than the vegetation but perhaps not by much. It did not even have a manse to offer the minister, and my new-lywed parents lived in a small apartment by the riverside. Life was not easy for them. They were on what is euphemistically called "minimum stipend" in the Presbyterian Church, which is church talk for "not much." But that was in truth the least of their problems. Their first child, a son named Paul, had been stillborn. Their second child, an infant daughter, Alana, was dying. She had been born with a hole in her heart, something that could be surgically repaired now but not in the Kootenays, not in the forties. My mother has told me that the baby cried and cried, and nothing they could do would comfort her. "Sometimes I can still hear her cry," said my mother. To make matters even worse, if that was possible, my mother had been terribly ill and was only slowly recovering from typhoid fever. Hard times indeed.

Just then my father decided to preach a sermon on the little story of Martha and Mary hosting Jesus. Dad told me that he let Martha have it right between the eyes with a homiletical two-by-four. Why didn't she have the sense to sit down and listen to Jesus? How dare she try to drag her sister away to the kitchen! Why did she think Jesus wanted another casserole rather than a disciple willing to listen to him? It was tough stuff, bluntly spoken. When the sermon was over, Dad took off his preaching gown, hung it in the closet and dragged himself off to the little apartment with the sick wife and the dying child.

Sitting at the door of the apartment was a casserole. On the casserole was a note. All that it said was "From Martha."

Dad said to me, "I never preached that sermon the same way again."

Lots of church folk, especially women, are made acutely uncomfortable by the story of Mary and Martha. Only a few will say out loud, "It's un-fair," but I am pretty sure that is what many others are thinking. They may not protest with the silent eloquence of the Martha in Trail, British Columbia, but they still don't want a preacher to take a homiletical two-by-four to them. What they do say is some variation on "Where would the church be without its Marthas?" And the answer, in all truth, is, in trouble." We all know that and my Dad learned, painfully, not to bash

Martha. So did I, from listening to the story. If I were preaching on the Mary and Martha story today, I could tell that story and say, "Whatever you do, don't be too hard on Martha. No two-by-fours!"

Still, Mary, not Martha, has made the better choice. There are times when the Christian faith is not about doing, doing, and doing some more. It is about sitting and listening. Every Christian—even Martha, especially Martha—needs a Mary point, a point of stillness close to Jesus. My old professor of ethics, Paul Lehmann, once preached a wonderful sermon, which I still remember forty years later, on a text drawn from *Alice in Wonderland*: "Don't just do something! Stand there." Stand there or sit there and let the grace of God catch up to you.

Stand there long enough to let the peace of Christ catch up to you. That is worth both teaching and learning.

A Coda

By the way, there's another little twist to the story. I was born in Ontario, in eastern Canada, after my parents left Trail. (I often wonder whether I was born healthy because they left Trail.) In 2003, however, I became the Dean of St. Andrew's Hall in Vancouver, British Columbia. Shortly thereafter Mary, one of the staff at St. Andrew's Hall, was attending a wedding in Calgary, Alberta. Before the service began, an older woman, perhaps in her seventies, leaned forward from her pew, tapped Mary on the shoulder, and said, "I understand you work at St. Andrew's Hall." Mary acknowledged this was true and the woman continued.

"How is Stephen Farris enjoying Vancouver?" she asked.

"Fine, I think," replied Mary. "Do you know Stephen?"

"I've never met him, but I grew up in Trail, and I remember the Farris family. They had such a hard time there, and my mother just loved them. She liked to look after them. In fact, I can remember taking a casserole to their apartment. I don't understand why but I remember she put a label on it, 'From Martha.'"

Among other things, stories call to mind in listeners similar stories from their own lives. We have all sat at tables where two storytellers compete for attention. Each story ends with a stare that silently shouts, top that! There are even storytellers who are so self-centered that they never allow stories or thoughts to flow from anyone else, but that need not happen. If the first storyteller genuinely makes psychological room at the table, those stories will pour out. Moreover, the stories that come in response will probably be related in some way to the original story. They will be a sign that the listener has internalized something from the story or, to put it another way, that teaching and learning has taken place. The story has been a human means of creating a "teachable spirit," which is a necessary precondition for gaining something of value from a sermon or lesson. If someone in the line shaking hands at the church door says something like, "Your sermon reminded me of something that happened to me..." that remark actually means something.

Moreover, because the two stories are related—that is, the story told by the preacher and the story told by the listener—something quite wonderful may happen. The relationship between the stories enhances the relationship among the people, both those who tell the stories and those who listen. So, for example:

Visiting Trail

Eventually the Presbyterian congregation in Trail purchased and thoroughly renovated a former Roman Catholic church no longer needed by the diocese. It was a sounder structure, in a more central and visible location, than the old Presbyterian church which, to be honest, had never fully recovered from being submerged in the great flood of 1948. In the spring of 2004 the work of renovation was done, and I was invited to preach both at the regular Sunday morning service of the congregation and at the formal opening of the new church on Sunday afternoon.

I cannot remember what I preached on either occasion, but I do remember telling the casserole story at one or the other service. (Even preachers remember stories but forget sermons!) It was 1949 when my parents left Trail, but in the reception after the service the older folks in the congregation, who still remembered them, headed directly to me, each with their own story.

One older lady told me about the Sunday my mother returned to church after her baby died. Mom had a beautiful alto singing voice and served as soloist in the church choir. Her normal seat was almost directly behind the pulpit. That Sunday was hardly normal, but nevertheless Mom took her accustomed seat. Early in the sermon she began to cry gently but steadily and without cease.

"Your father reached behind himself and took her hand. He preached the entire sermon holding her hand."

Another lady told me, "Your parents used to walk down to the old bridge over the Columbia River. They would stand side by side with a bag of roasted sunflower seeds, lean over the bridge, and spit the hulls of the seeds into the water."

After the reception, my wife, Patty, and I climbed in our car, and, after receiving careful directions, drove up the mountain to the cemetery. We found the graves of my brother ("A Jewel for His Crown," says the tiny headstone) and my sister ("A Lamb for His Keeping.") Together we stood on the close cropped cemetery grass and imagined a young couple—younger at that point even than our own son, also named Allan, and his wife, Judith—so very young, clinging to each other by the graves of their children. But with the help of friends, especially the support of the rector of St. Andrew's Anglican Church, who took them under his wing, they survived. They turned from those graves and made their way back down the mountainside and back down to life. That's the hardest part of any funeral I think. It's the moment that you have to turn away from the body of the one you love—and turn back to life. Patty and I turned away from the graves and made our way back down the hill also.

It says something about Trail and its people that despite these memories, my mother and father always spoke of the town and their time there with a smile in their eyes. A town and its people have to be very special for that to happen. So Patty pulled her cell phone from her purse, and we phoned Mom. We told her exactly where we were, and as we drove through town Mom's memories poured out. We would tell her what corner we had reached, and she would remember what had stood there in the old days. She recalled where her special friends lived, which stores were where, and guided us to the block where their apartment had been located.

With a slightly embarrassed laugh she admitted, "Some evenings your father and I used to take a bag of sunflower seeds down to the bridge. We would lean over and spit seeds into the current. Not very dignified behavior for the Presbyterian minister and his wife! But, of course, nobody ever knew about it."

"Mom, they knew!" I told her.

Ministers have no secrets in small towns. In a small town they know, they always know.

Here's another family story:

Snow Blind

In the very early years of the twentieth century my homesteader grandfather,
Charles Allan Farris, then a young man, would walk the seventy miles to
Fort Battleford to fetch the mail to the village of Coleville where he lived. The
western plains of Canada can be bitterly cold in the winter so that once the
snow arrives it stays until road construction season. The prairies are, how-
ever, also very dry so there are many bright winter days when the sun shines
unimpeded onto the dazzlingly reflective fields of snow. That combination can
easily bring on snow blindness, a temporary condition caused by the excess
of light. So it was with my grandfather, returning from Fort Battleford one
winter's day with the village's mail. He went blind with the excess of light
and had to crawl the rest of the way home, feeling for the edge of the path
with his hands.

This kind of story can be used to teach, in a sermon on, for example, the logos hymn of John 1. Sometimes when thinking and speaking of God, especially with respect to the great themes of creation and eternity, I feel like my grandfather, blind from the excess of light, feeling my way along an uncertain path with my hands. That sense of the otherness and transcendence of God is a great truth and is central to the Christian faith. Among other things, without a sense of God's otherness and transcendence, we lose our sense of the miracle of the incarnation. God becomes the kindly "man upstairs" and Christmas merely cute. At the very least, stories impart truth, a concept we will not define philosophically here. Why? Because listeners to stories know that they are touched on a level and sometimes even persuaded in a way that philosophical discourse seldom achieves. Our hearts are more likely to be "strangely warmed" by a story than a proposition or a treatise. Stories at their best do more than illustrate an otherwise abstract truth; they cause truth to grow within us and grasp us. That, with the aid of the Holy Spirit, is precisely what the gospel stories do, and our stories, by grace, can sometimes imitate them.

The story "Snow Blind" was told to me by my father when I was only a boy. But a number of years ago I received a privately printed history of that Saskatchewan village and township. The same story was in the history, but it was told about another pioneer, not Charles Allan Farris. Obviously the story migrated from one family to another, but I do not know for sure the direction of the migration. I am doubtless prejudiced but I think that the Farris family version is likely the more accurate. In the first place, my late father was closer to the event than the author of the local history. Moreover, he was a historically trained academic and thus likely to be more careful about accuracy. I also think a big, strong man like my grandfather would have been more likely than most to have the physical strength actually to survive the ordeal. Finally, the Farris family had moved away from the township, and it seems to me likely that under those circumstances a good anecdote like this one would be adopted by some other family in order to keep it in the community. But I, of course, am a prejudiced observer. The problem is now at least a century old and almost certainly beyond resolution.

But let me lay the problem aside for a moment to ask a question: Is the truth of the insight affected by whether the pioneer was my grandfather or someone else?

By the way, this is a problem with respect to a much more familiar story than the one about my grandfather's snow blindness. Consider the verse 2 Sam 21:19: *"Then there was another battle with the Philistines at Gob; and Elhanan son of Jaare-oregim, the Bethlehemite, killed Goliath the Gittite, the shaft of whose spear was like a weaver's beam."*

There is, of course, another and much more familiar version of the story. So, who killed Goliath? The problem is now three millennia old, and almost certainly beyond resolution. Is the truth and the value of the story affected by who killed Goliath?

Sometimes stories teach by raising a question. Here is an example:

The U-Boat

Some time ago I was called to jury duty in Toronto. In our system, a panel of, as I recall, 120 prospective jurors is called up for a two-week period. From time to time the entire panel is called into courtrooms where individual panel members may be selected actually to serve on a jury. The rest of the time the panel sits in a large and not particularly comfortable waiting room. As you can imagine, people get quite territorial in such situations and always sit in the same place. I sat between a female Jewish psychologist and an older German man, obviously of World War II vintage. The two were intensely suspicious of one another. Whenever one was out of the room, the other would question me.

"Do you think he was in the SS?"

"No, I don't think so."

"Is she asking questions about me?"

I bent the truth in my response.

I felt caught in the middle, like Poland.

In fact, I was confident that the German man had not been in the SS but the U-boat service since he was reading a German-language magazine for veterans of the Unterseebootsmarine. On one of the occasions the psychologist was absent, he told me how he had come to Canada.

He said that the U-boat service had the highest casualty rate of any branch of the German military, about 75 percent dead. This rate was enormously high at the end of the war when Allied power was simply overwhelming. Sometime in the winter of 1945, perhaps February or March, the boat on which this man was serving as engineer pulled out to sea. (Submarines are boats, not ships, by the way.) When the boat was well clear of land, the captain gathered the officers together and announced, "Boys, this war is as good as over. I have no intention of getting us all killed in the last days of a lost war."

He sailed the boat across the Atlantic, carefully avoiding all Allied shipping. He settled the boat down on the bottom near Halifax, the main East Coast convoy port of Canada. (Take a look at a map, and you'll see why Halifax was used to gather the convoys. It is significantly farther east than the chief East Coast ports of the United States.) The point of this is that many wrecks happened in that area, and it would have been very difficult to distinguish one metal mass sitting still on the bottom from another. For about fifty days the boat sat there. Every night it would surface to replenish its oxygen, charge its batteries, and listen for the announcement that the war was over. Finally, that day came. The U-boat hoisted a white flag and waited outside the harbor to surrender. (Sometime later when I was in Halifax, I asked about the story and was told that a tugboat accepted the surrender.)

The prisoners were put in a train and transferred halfway across the country to a POW camp in the Canadian Shield country near Gravenhurst, Ontario. As the train traveled, the young engineer looked out the window and decided the new land in the bloom of spring and most of all, untouched by the ravages of war, was the most beautiful country he had ever seen. He was, of course, repatriated in due time and then began the process of immigration. Eventually he came to Canada, got a job in the parks department of one of the suburban municipalities in the Toronto area, and made a life for himself and his family as a Canadian citizen. In the course of his duties as a citizen, he found himself sitting next to me waiting to serve as a juror.

That's the story. I don't think that there is much doubt that the skipper's conduct and that of his officers would certainly constitute desertion, and in a court of military justice could well have been punishable by death in most nations. In Nazi Germany it would have certainly been a matter for the death penalty. But others might think he behaved with wisdom and humanity and very probably saved the lives of all his officers and men. The story raises questions worth thinking about, a key part of good teaching.

Here's an aside: reactions to this story may differ based on one's gender or nationality. I have not told this story frequently enough to generalize, but in my admittedly limited experience, women quickly affirm that the skipper did the right thing. In fact, they may come to that conclusion so quickly that the teaching value of the story is limited. Questions are not effectively raised if everyone immediately agrees on the answer. Canadian men generally come to the same conclusion but more slowly and deliberately. I also shared this story on a private Internet board where all the other participants are American men, a number of them military veterans. The reaction there was very different, with the veterans in particular thinking that the call of duty remained paramount even under those circumstances. The thing to learn here is not that women are different from men or Canadians from Americans, though both may be true. It is that the background of listeners must be taken into account when considering the likely listener response to a story.

But stories can be useful in raising questions.

Stories also offer direct moral instruction. Think of Aesop's fables, such as "The Hare and the Tortoise." These effectively teach us that "slow and steady wins the race" or other morals. As I look over my own stock of stories, I realize that few, if any, offer unambiguous instruction (though "Appointment in Samarra" and perhaps even "The Socks," which will appear next, may come close). Stories that unambiguously set forth examples for us to follow are the most likely to become tedious for listeners. Theologically, this is because many of them easily become moralistic. This is especially the case with children's stories, in my experience. A distressingly large number of them seem to have the message, children, God wants you to be nice. Such stories set up an example, challenge us to follow it, and, furthermore, make the assumption that we can indeed imitate the example. The truth is, however, that we may not be able to follow the example. "I do not do what I want, but I do the very thing I hate" (Rom 7:15). How likely is it that most of us can emulate the self-sacrifice of, say, Mother Teresa? Moreover, example stories may implicitly suggest that Christianity is primarily about what we must or must not do rather than about what God has done and will do for us by grace through Jesus Christ and the work of the Holy Spirit. No doubt, however, one function of stories, even of ones that verge on the tedious, is to instruct.[6]

The line between instruction and persuasion is blurred with respect to stories. Stories can function both to show us what is right and declare what is wrong, and also to persuade us to do the one or avoid the other. Still, it is clear that one useful function of stories is to persuade.

Stories Persuade

In ancient rhetoric, persuasion is the most important of the three functions. Aristotle even defined rhetoric as "the faculty of observing in any given case the available means of persuasion."[7] This may have been because the chief end of an education in rhetoric was to fit the young person (almost always a man) for distinction in the assemblies of the ancient world or as an advocate in the courts, or both. Such rhetoric was categorized as either deliberative (that is, designed to persuade an assembly to undertake a certain course of action) or forensic (that is, designed to convince judges and courts in legal proceedings). The motivation to learn to persuade was straightforward: You will not have a successful career in politics if fellow legislators doze off as soon as you begin speaking, or in law if you cannot persuade a court that your client is not guilty! So learn to speak well!

A third category of rhetoric, namely *epideictic*, had to do with honour or blame on ceremonial occasions, such as in a funeral oration. This may have been a more significant function in the ancient world; though, come to think of it, a minister who can't do a good funeral is still in trouble, especially in a small town.

In contemporary preaching or, of course, teaching, instruction appears to be the foremost of the three functions of rhetoric. Hence, instruction may be likewise the chief contemporary function of stories. This function is readily recognized and accepted in contemporary preaching and teaching. Teachers of preaching are, by contrast, often ambivalent about persuasion. The great teacher of preaching Richard Lischer wrote

6. Such stories function as the *paradeigma* or "paradigms" of Aristotle's *Rhetoric*.

7. Aristotle, *Rhetoric*, Book 1.2.

a marvelously titled essay, "Why I Am Not Persuasive," on this very subject.[8] The argument of the essay has been challenged. In the same issue
of the journal in which it first appeared, it was paired with another essay
offering a more positive view of persuasion. Lischer's essay has, however,
proved widely influential, which, ironically enough, is a different way
of saying that many have found it persuasive. I may be counted in that
number.

For the purposes of this book, however, we can lay aside the debate
for a time. After all, most preachers and teachers hope that something
will happen as a result of what they say. Some preachers hope some listeners will commit their lives to the Lord Jesus Christ, and that others
will renew their commitment. Some preachers hope that their listeners
will increase their commitment to justice and perhaps even invest their
time, energy, and money in a particular cause. Or any kind of preacher
or teacher will hope that their listeners will behave in certain ways in
their personal or family lives. And, clearly, preachers do use stories in the
expectation that the stories will help this happen.

Persuasion is the function of rhetoric that is fraught with danger
and that has been held in suspicion for millennia. The debate about the
use of persuasion in preaching is a particular Christian instance of an
argument that goes back at least to Socrates and the Sophists and was
doubtless brought into Christianity a mere heartbeat after the importa-
tion of rhetoric itself. The debate cannot be resolved or even adequately
described here.

The crux of the issue, however, is that there is much room for manipulation here. If stories are used to manipulate listeners, it is shameful.
People are rightly brought to a saving knowledge of Jesus Christ and a
lasting commitment to him because of the work of the Holy Spirit im-
printing the gospel on their hearts. If they become committed to justice
or behave more decently with their families, it ought to be because that
same Holy Spirit is at work in their hearts, not because a preacher or
teacher has played with their emotions by telling stories. Why people do
what they do still matters. T. S. Eliot was right: "The last act is the greatest
treason: / to do the right deed for the wrong reason."[9] It may even be that
the task of the preacher or teacher is not at all to persuade but to lay out

---

8. Lischer, "Why I Am not Persuasive." A counterpoint essay may be found in the
same issue of the journal *Homiletic*: Hogan, "Rethinking Persuasion."

9. Eliot, *Murder in the Cathedral*, 47.

the truth in Christ and leave the question of whether anybody acts on it to God. There is a certain appropriate humility in such an attitude.

The limitations of the categories we have been using appear at this point. Delight, though real, is not enough. We do wish to instruct, but instruction is not sufficient for an unrepentant heart. Persuasion as such may also be too small a category. We do not want to win an argument; we want to win a person. It still may actually be closer to the chief end of preaching, however. Ultimately, the aim of the sermon is not primarily to convey ideas but to evoke an experience of the gospel.[10] We hope, humbly and dependent on the work of the Holy Spirit, that Christ will be formed in the lives of our listeners. Such lives are, far more than sermons, lessons or stories, the best witness to the gospel. We may even hope, very humbly indeed, that our words may help this to happen. If that happens, it is close to persuasion.

It was considered in rhetoric that persuasion could take place in three ways. These were identified as *logos, pathos,* and *ethos. Logos* had to do with rational argument, especially the syllogisms beloved by ancient philosophers.[11] Formal syllogisms may be rare in contemporary preaching and teaching, but rational argument still has its place. We might argue, for example, that attending worship regularly as a family is good for family unity. (Yes, that kind or argument can reduce the worship of God to a mere means to an end and make the apparent health of the family more important than acknowledging the glory of God. But that observation, though important, would be beside the point of this paragraph.) We might then introduce statistics to back the claim. Stories, especially factual, nonfiction ones, come into this mode of persuasion as examples of the truth of the claim.

Pathos has to do with an appeal to the emotions of the listeners. Speakers both ancient and contemporary know the efficacy of an appeal to the emotions. This is the mode of persuasion in which stories are most obviously useful—and also most open to the charge of listener manipulation. Using a story as part of a *pathos* appeal, is much safer if it is in the service of an argument that can also be advanced by means of *logos.*

10. Reid et al., "Preaching as the Creation of an Experience." The authors were making this claim about the "new homiletic." I think the claim could be extended to preaching in general.

11. In practice the full syllogism was often replaced by a shorter, simpler version called the *enthymeme.* In an enthymeme a term of the syllogism was left unstated, to be supplied by the listener.

Ethos has to do with the apparent character of the speaker. An audience is far more likely to allow a speaker who appears trustworthy to persuade them. Note that what matters in *ethos* is not quite the actual character of the speaker but the character of the speaker as perceived by the audience. It is likely that an audience will listen carefully to someone who appears to share the values and aspirations of the listeners. Whether this appearance of sharing is true or not is not actually certain. Long before I ever read about of these modes of persuasion, I used *ethos* arguments unconsciously. For example, if I were speaking in a Baptist church, I would emphasize my Baptist connections and my experience speaking in other Baptist churches. What I would really be saying is, "Even though I am a Presbyterian, you good Baptists can still trust me!"

In fact, especially in matters where a conclusion is doubtful and hard to achieve by other means, *ethos* was considered the most effective mode of persuasion. That may still be the case. Think of the ads that inundate the airways during an election campaign. Very few, if any, even attempt to argue logically the merits of a candidate's position. The positive ads, rather, try to show us that the candidate shares the values and goals of the majority of the electorate, that the candidate is a patriot or a family person or someone who understands how hard it is for a person like you to make ends meet. You can trust that person because he or she is the kind of person you can imagine sitting down with to have a friendly chat. The attack ads, which seem to proliferate more with every election, are, on the other hand, an exercise in negative *ethos*. One side claims that the opposing candidate is a thoroughgoing liberal or a tax-and-spend socialist. From the other side of the political divide come ads that attempt to show that the opponent is a right-wing whacko or a dangerous warmonger. The real message in both cases is, that person is not like you, and is not trustworthy. Very smart advertising agencies spend millions of dollars on such ads because they know they work. The ancients were right. *Ethos* persuades.

There is a problem in all this for Christian preachers and teachers. We are supposed to point not to ourselves but to Christ. While character certainly does matter in communication, we are not in the business of trying to demonstrate that we are like our listeners. Our task is, as nearly as possible, to ensure that our actual rather than our apparent character is like Jesus. And there is no guarantee that being like Jesus will make us more believable. Lots of people did not believe Jesus. His character, among other things, got him crucified. Being like Jesus may not "work" as well as trying to appear to be like our listeners. But this a matter that can be better discussed in a later chapter.

Our point in all this is that the stories we relate tell our listeners a great deal about us as speakers. Perhaps our stories may tell even more about us as speakers than about the supposed subject of our address. The results can be either positive or negative. By this point, for example, some readers may be already beginning to have some notions about my character. Some will be more ready to believe what I say about storytelling because I seem to be the kind of person who can be trusted. Others may be ready to shut the book for good. That's *ethos*.

The Socks

A number of years ago, when I was still teaching in Toronto, I had a student named Jeff. He was a fine preacher and, a fact relevant to the story, a tall man. That winter Jeff was preaching in a church temporarily without a minister, located in a small Ontario city, but nevertheless large enough to have both a downtown and the problems often associated with downtowns. One Sunday following a bitterly cold Saturday night, Jeff was sitting in the minister's vacant study, putting the final touches on his sermon.

Just then a church lady, the kind they used to parody on Saturday Night Live, bustled in looking both agitated and determined. "Jeff! There's a homeless person in the church and he stinks. You're a big man. I want you to come and throw him out." Determined church ladies can be difficult to say no to, especially if they are agitated, so Jeff decided to follow her into the church.

Jeff followed the church lady into the sanctuary and sure enough, there was indeed a homeless person in the front pew. And she was quite right; he did stink. He smelt as if he had passed the night in a dumpster which was, when you think about it, quite possibly the exact truth. A dumpster would cut the winter wind, after all. His clothes were shabby, torn, and stained, and his shoes were cracked and down at heel. Worst of all, in that bitter Ontario winter, he had no socks and his ankles were blue with the cold.

It happened, and this too is relevant to the story, that the sermon that day was to be drawn from Jesus's parable of the final judgment. In that parable, the righteous come before the Master and he says, "Come, you that are blessed by my Father, inherit the kingdom prepared for you from the foundation of the world; for I was hungry and you gave me food, I was thirsty and you gave me something to drink, I was a stranger and you welcomed me, I was naked and you gave me clothing, I was sick and you took care of me, I was in prison and you visited me." They are surprised by this, of course, and so they say, "Lord, when was it that we saw you hungry and gave you food, or thirsty and gave you something to drink?"

The King replies, "'Truly I tell you, just as you did it to one of the least of these who are members of my family, you did it to me."

Now, when the unrighteous come before the Master, of course, he says . . . but you can probably figure that out for yourselves.

So, when Jeff looked at the homeless man, it was as if he could hear the Master saying to him personally, "I had no socks and my ankles were blue with the cold, and you threw me out into the frozen winter."

He was just working up the courage to say "No" to the church lady when he realized that she was not the only kind of church lady in that congregation. Another, very different, church lady had fixed some sandwiches for the man. The clerk of session, the chief elder of the church, was sitting beside the man in the front pew and conversing with him, almost as if he were a real human being, and a guest in their church, worthy of courtesy and respect! Best of all, Jeff told me, a small girl, perhaps seven or eight years old, came up to the homeless man and handed him a pair of rolled-up men's socks.

"Jeff," I said, "that's a wonderful story. May I use it?"

"Surely," he replied politely. Students are normally polite to their professors!

But even as I asked, I realized there was one little detail I didn't understand, and I do like to get the details right if I am going to tell a story. "Where did the socks come from? Is there a 'clothes closet' for the needy in that congregation?" I asked. Many churches, especially in downtown locations, collect clothes for the needy, and perhaps there was a supply of clothes, including socks, on hand. That would explain it.

"No, there isn't," said Jeff, "and I don't know where the socks came from."

Now, I don't know where the socks came from either, but here's a guess. It's the only answer I can imagine, but it's still just a guess.

I think the little girl got the socks from her father. Where else could she find them? I think there was a little girl in that church with the love of God in her heart. And I think there was a very proud father with a warm heart . . . and cold feet.

For many years when I told this story I changed Jeff's name, a useful practice in many cases. However, Jeff died recently of a virulent form of cancer that came upon him with startling rapidity. I had a lengthy conversation with Jeff shortly before he fell ill and, among other things, verified the details of the story with him. I have therefore changed the name back to the real name of Rev. Jeff Veenstra, a fine man and an expert preacher of the gospel.

One can never fully predict how listeners, or in this case readers, will react, but the sermon must speak first to the preacher. That story still speaks to me after many years and my heart is warmed every time I think of it. Now, it could certainly be used to persuade a congregation towards specific actions, to contribute generously to an out-of-the-cold program, for example. But that is too limited an act of persuasion. What preachers and teachers may hope for in telling stories is that the heart, and not merely the feet, may be "strangely warmed."

2

The Five Skills of the Storyteller

Being able to tell a good story is not enough. The ability to tell a tale is but one of at least five different skills of the storyteller. It may be a relief to hear that being able to make up a story is not one of those five skills.

Wilde Wit

There is an old story about the great Irish wit Oscar Wilde. He once heard someone else deliver a superlatively witty line and said, "I wish I had said that!" A friend, knowing Wilde's nature, assured him, "You will, Oscar. You will!"

We imitate Oscar Wilde in that respect, borrowing our stories from a vast common-property fund of stories out there. There is nothing inherently wrong with this. (See chapter 4, on the ethics of storytelling, however!) That kind of borrowing is the sincerest form of flattery. If a story is any good, you will want to retell it yourself, whether in a sermon, a classroom, or simply at your own table. And that is what most of us do, retell stories. Most of us are in the retell end of the story business, not the manufacturing side.

Very few of us can actually compose good stories of our own. If we could do so, we would likely be famous authors. From time to time I hear or read statements by professors of New Testament about the parables in the Gospels, asserting airily that they somehow "arose in the community" of the early church. It makes me wonder if the professors have actually ever tried to compose a parable. I do not mean updating an old parable: "A man was travelling from New York to Buffalo," for example. I am referring to composing an entirely new one. I once took on the task of composing a parable as an experiment. The chief thing I found was that it is exceedingly difficult, and I am quite sure that not many would bother remembering the result in my case. People with rare gifts compose parables, and that is true for stories in general. There is not many a Garrison Keillor out there, to pick one example. That need not stop us from telling stories, however.

To shift direction slightly: how many of us ever make up jokes? What we actually do is hear good jokes, store them away in our memory, and then produce them at the right opportunity. At least, we hope it is the right opportunity. There is very little more painful to listeners than the wrong joke at the wrong time. Or, for that matter, the wrong story in the wrong sermon. But remarkably few of us ever actually make up a joke. So it is with stories. The truly useful skill for a preacher or teacher to develop is recognizing a good story when we hear or read one and sensing how it may be used. An extension of that skill is witnessing a situation and recognizing that, with a little kneading and shaping, it can be turned into a good story. If I claim any skill for myself, it is only this: I think I do have the eye or ear for a situation that can be turned into a story. I do not expect of my readers, therefore, what I can only rarely do myself, which is to actually create a story. What most of us can do, however, is the narrative equivalent of joke telling, recognizing a good one when we hear it and passing it on at the right moment. That leads to yet another skill, creating a way of saving the story so it can be retrieved at the right moment.

The actual skill of telling a story in a vigorous and interesting manner is surely vital, but it is only one facet of the storyteller's art. At least five different skills are necessary for the storyteller:

1. Recognizing a potential story.

2. Knowing when (and when not) to use a story.

3. Telling the story in an effective way.

4. Linking the story appropriately to the rest of the sermon or lesson.

5. Organizing and storing stories so they can be retrieved later.

1. RECOGNIZING A POTENTIAL STORY

The internet is full of stories for preachers and teachers. In the old days there were books of stories published for the anxious preacher, and the most common question directed to professors of homiletics might have been, "Heard any good stories lately?" Preachers and teachers have always wanted to find stories of one sort or another. Now the internet seems to be the source of many of the tales that appear in sermons and lessons. But many stories will come to us if we merely keep our eyes and ears open, and these stories will often be more compelling and authentic than the ones we find on the internet. They will often have an air of vigor missing from the overused tales extracted from the internet.

Most of the stories in this book were recognized rather than composed. To illustrate the process, let's consider an anecdote that I will attempt to develop into a story that can be used in a sermon. The skills listed above are all part of this process of working with an observation in which so little happens that it is barely a story at all according to our working definition. But it all starts with taking notice, which is skill number 1. So here is an observation from a crowded car on the Toronto subway system. It is, I think, an unpromising anecdote at first sight and, to be honest, is fraught with difficulties. Much more striking and unusual events have happened in my life. These were easy to recognize and, for that matter, to retell as stories. This incident, however, is more like a regular happening if we take time to notice. If you wish to get the story as a whole, you will find it later in this chapter. Here, however, it will be separated into stages of development.

In Toronto subway cars a particular kind of two-person seat extends perpendicularly into the body of the car. The outer seat of the two is the one that offers a jumbo-sized person, such as myself, the seat with the greatest possible useable legroom. I remember a rush hour when I actually managed to nab that seat. Next to me was a man short enough that, standing, he was only a little taller than I am, sitting. He was very slightly built and fine-boned, wore Coke-bottle-thick, gold-wire-rimmed glasses, and was trying to grow what was in truth a very wispy mustache. Now, there is nothing at all wrong with ~ll. Among other things, small people live longer than men my size, ~ing is, however, that he was reading a book, which due to and the crowded subway car was almost thrust in my face. ning through Intimidation."

It all starts with taking notice and recognizing the possibilities that lie in a particular observation. Other skills must also be brought to bear before this could become a helpful story in a sermon, but the first step is recognition. The particular characteristic that makes this observation worth thinking about is incongruity. Like it or not, a man of the physical characteristics named in the story is at a disadvantage in the intimidation department. This brings me to the first problem in turning the observation into a story for a sermon, one that may be a particular challenge to me. I am the size of a retired offensive tackle, and if I were to turn this observation into a sermon story, I may appear to be mocking small people. I certainly don't intend to, but I might easily be perceived as doing so. That very real possibility could be diminished by telling the story with the right vocal tone, facial expression, and body language—all matters that cannot be represented on the page here but that nevertheless are very important. They are, in fact, part of skill number 3 listed at the beginning of the chapter: telling the story in an effective way. It is better, however, to name the difficulty aloud, as you can see in my description of the small man. I note, however, that the right response might have been not to tell the story at all but rather to hit the homiletical delete button. The decision whether or not to use an observation to create a sermon story is skill number 2 above.

2. KNOWING WHEN (AND WHEN NOT) TO USE A STORY

Sometimes stories are simply not worth telling in a sermon.

I remember hearing a student preach a sermon that included a lengthy story about a traveller climbing Mount Washington in New Hampshire in a snowstorm. Apparently Mount Washington has a broad, flat summit, and somewhere on that summit there is a climbers' shelter. The unfortunate climber in the story wandered around and around in the snowstorm, unable to find his way to the shelter, and eventually died of exposure and sheer exhaustion. As far as I can remember, the story had only the most tenuous of connections with the rest of the sermon and, in any case, it's hardly one of those cheerful tales that lift the spirits of the congregation. In truth, the story was a fitting metaphor for what happened to the sermon that day. It too wandered around until it died.

I have been reliably informed that the same student told a children's story about the good things Adolf Hitler did. My guess is that this little tale may well have puzzled the four- and five-year-olds surrounding him on the chancel steps. It certainly caused the jaws of the adults in the congregation, some of whom had suffered greatly in World War II, to drop to somewhere near the hymnbook racks. Some stories simply should not be told. Now, this is not to deny that a great preacher might figure out some creative way to use the Mount Washington story in a sermon. But the rest of us would be better off leaving it out—and our listeners would be better never hearing it.

Although a sermon might include a story that should never be told or heard, a sermon might more often include a story that's good in itself but that doesn't really belong. This happens frequently to preachers and teachers who hear a wonderful story and say to themselves, "Great story! I need to fit that in this week." They get out their homiletical crowbar and wedge it in no matter what. It would be far better for both the sermon and the story to save the story for another sermon. If it actually is a good story but either does not fit the overall content of a sermon or comes at the wrong time in a sermon, then it will probably overshadow the surrounding material. People will remember the story and not whatever else the preacher is trying to say. If it is a mediocre story or worse—perhaps a story about the good things Hitler did—it simply leaves puzzlement. If a preacher does this often enough, puzzlement eventually becomes mockery, and phone calls to the church authorities are not far behind. Knowing when and when not to tell a story is a key skill.

3. TELLING THE STORY IN AN EFFECTIVE WAY

As I suggested above, the ability to tell as story is of first importance. This skill is, however, better learned live, and not from a book. The best way to learn to tell stories is to listen to good stories and then to start telling stories yourself. (Don't just read; also listen! Reading stories is good; listening is better.) For example, in telling the story "The Luckiest Man in Canada," which appears in chapter 1, a good storyteller will pause just before the key line, "And I married the nurse!" It is better to hear that than to read about it, however. Two obvious starting places are the stories of Garrison Keillor and Stuart McLean. Keillor's Lake Wobegon stories can be found in print or audio books, and McLean's stories are available on the Canadian Broadcasting Corporation (CBC) website. Ask yourself, what made that story compelling, and how can I make the stories I tell as riveting?

Very little could be as boring as reading a disquisition on the skills of storytelling, and it is not my intention to offer one. From time to time, however, I will point out some of the compositional aspects of storytelling, as they appear in the stories in this book.

4. LINKING THE STORY APPROPRIATELY TO THE REST OF THE SERMON OR LESSON

So far the observation about the small man and his book, *Winning through Intimidation*, isn't quite a story, as defined in this book: This observation has some important hints of character, but nothing has happened, and no choices are made. In short, there isn't yet a plot to intersect with character. I need to add something therefore both to make the observation into a story and to link it to a sermon or lesson. Here is what I did add to turn it into a story.

I felt like telling him, "It won't work!" But I didn't. I thought I might scare him.

Now, at least, something has happened. I made a choice not to challenge the man about his choice of reading material. At the first level, this observation, which was now a story, worked. The congregation laughed heartily, but laughter was certainly not my aim in telling the story. It actually reinforces the danger that I might seem to be mocking the man. I also have not yet linked it to the Scripture text or to the rest of the sermon. Sometimes leaving a story uninterpreted may be the best choice. Jesus's parables are often left uninterpreted, though the gospel writers certainly present their own subtle interpretations by their placement of the parables within each gospel. Placing a parable in a particular narrative context is an act of interpretation in itself. Our stories too will frequently need to be linked to the rest of the sermon and interpreted at least by their position in the sermon. From time to time, we must admit, our stories are not that interesting in themselves. Sometimes it the link to the rest of the sermon or lesson, or, to phrase it differently, the way a story is used, that makes the stories interesting. The way a speaker uses a story might be more interesting than the story itself.

Everything is connected to everything else, and if you work very hard, you can probably create some kind of connection between that story and almost any text . . . if you work at it very, very hard indeed. Your listeners may need to work nearly as hard, however, and that is rarely a good thing.

Perhaps a clever preacher could figure out a connection between my story and the biblical story of the call of the disciples, to pick a Scripture passage out of the air. But the connection in such a case is likely not very clear. In this case, I felt I needed a more explicit interpretation and link to the day's text so that listeners could recognize without excessive strain where I was going.

Actually the whole thing saddened me. I knew with 100 percent moral certainty that the small man had himself been intimidated, probably regularly, and had come to the terrible conclusion that the way ahead in life was to imitate his persecutors. But Jesus says that's wrong, even if it does work. The people who "win through intimidation," may get the promotions and the big salary. But they won't inherit the earth; the meek will.

And the small man, has a chance to be among them . . . though it would help if he read the Gospel of Matthew instead of Winning through Intimidation.

So what does the word *meek* mean? Sometimes it's easier to start with the negative. I don't think it means "doormat." It doesn't even mean the classic Canadian thing of apologizing if somebody steps on your foot. It may partly be a matter of a particular social situation. The quiet, ordinary folks who never make a big noise about themselves and never make the lifestyles of the rich and famous, except possibly as a chambermaid in the background, may be the meek.

5. ORGANIZING AND STORING STORIES SO THEY CAN BE RETRIEVED AT A LATER POINT

Stories are immensely powerful, and in such cases, they have the capacity to overshadow the surrounding material. Listeners remember the story and forget the sermon together with whatever conceptual material it was designed to convey. To refrain from telling the story seems an overreaction, however. What is more sensible is to be sure that the story and the rest of the sermon or lecture actually work together rather than against each other. The preacher or teacher needs to learn the patience to wait for the right time and the right occasion to tell the story. If we simply trust our memories, however, it is very likely that we will be unable to recall the story at the right time to use it.

All this means that a storyteller needs to develop some system of storing, labeling, and categorizing by subject matter and possible Scripture text so that she can use a story at the right time. Consider this, if you will, the storytelling equivalent of establishing a wine cellar. It is a good thing to be able to pull a bottle, or a story, from the cellar at the right time. And some stories, like wine, can be the better for aging.

In former times, ministers used to do this manually. I recall my superb supervisor from my intern year in a West Virginia church, Dr. Dean Thomson, telling and showing me how, once a quarter, he went through his magazines and newspapers, clipping out stories and phrases to be filed manually in folders. Some people may still find that the best procedure. Most of us, however, will use a computer. The real question is how to do it. Computer software changes so fast, and my own skills are so limited that I will not speak about the mechanics of keeping this kind of filing system here. Whether you use a database or simply your word processor is up to you. Most of my readers will have more advanced skills than I possess. It should be noted that your system can certainly hold more than stories. My own file of stories has more or less turned into this book but I also keep a folder on my computer called "Commonplace." In former days, many people kept what was usually called a commonplace book. They wrote into their commonplace books snippets of thoughts (very often about spiritual matters), poems, well-phrased quotations, observations, and anything else that struck them. My computer folder has very much the same function for me. Some of these thoughts do make their way into sermons or lectures. Whether or not that is the case, they have made their way into my heart.

A further advantage to creating a database of stories and observations is that it allows us to estimate the cumulative effect of the stories we tell and the other materials we pass on to our listeners. One story or observation will likely only have a limited effect on listeners. If we harp on the same themes repeatedly, however, they do get through, for better or for worse. If, for example, all our stories are about women and men who do great things for God, or about our failure to do what we ought to do for God, we will inevitably be communicating the notion that the Christian faith is about what we must do and, moreover, that we are miserable failures at our end of the relationship. To use the categories of the apostle Paul, to communicate this would be to preach law rather than gospel.

Let us return to my story about the man on the training reading *Winning through Intimidation.* The interpretation I lay out above also is a major clue to the use of skill number 5: organizing and storing stories so they can be retrieved later. In the first place, I need to give the story a title that will recall the story to my memory. The two characteristics of such a title should be that it is short and that it recalls the substance of the story to my memory. It doesn't need to be brilliant or witty, though that would not hurt. It just needs to be recognizable. I have already used the title I did eventually select, "Winning through Intimidation."

An aside here: I made an error at this point that was only caught on about the fifth edit. I first wrote, "Winning through Interpretation." For the preacher, teacher and storyteller, that may be generally true. That is indeed how we "win."

A good title may be enough in your filing system. Something else may eventually be helpful, however. I might choose to save the story under a possible biblical text or texts and by subject. I might save my story "Winning through Intimidation" under Matt 5:5, or, more generally, under "Beatitudes" or under "Meek"—or, indeed, under all three.

Here is a pointer that came to me from a student who is much more computer savvy than I am. She reminded me that many of the materials we put in our database will likely come from the internet. They need not only be stories. They may also be reflections, quotations, or video clips of many sorts. It makes sense to include the link to the URL of whatever it is that is being saved. However, web pages do disappear, and links go inactive. It is wise to cut and paste written materials into the database itself and to write a sufficient description of video clips so that you can remember what they were some months or years later.

Here then is the story as a whole as it might appear in my personal repository of stories.

Winning through Intimidation

Matthew 5:5

Beatitudes, Meek

In Toronto subway cars, a kind of two-person seat extends perpendicularly into the body of the car. The outer seat of the two is the one that offers a jumbo-sized person, such as myself, the seat with the greatest possible legroom. I remember a particular rush hour when I actually managed to get that seat. Next to me was a man short enough that, standing, he was only a little taller than I am, sitting. He was very slightly built, fine boned, wore thick, gold wire rimmed glasses, and was trying to grow what was, in truth, a very wispy mustache. Now, there is nothing at all wrong with being small. Among other things, small people live longer than men my size, on average. The thing is, however, that he was reading a book, which due to our relative heights and the crowded subway car, was almost thrust in my face. The title was "Winning through Intimidation."

I felt like telling him, "It won't work!" But I didn't. I thought I might scare him.

Actually the whole thing saddened me. I knew with 100 percent moral certainty that the small man had himself been intimidated, probably regularly, and had come to the terrible conclusion that the way ahead in life was to imitate his persecutors. But Jesus says that's wrong, even if it does work. The people who "win through intimidation," may get the promotions and the big salary. But they won't inherit the earth; the meek will. And the small man, has a chance to be among them . . . though it would help if he read the Gospel of Matthew instead of Winning through Intimidation.

So what does the word meek *mean? Sometimes it's easier to start with the negative. I don't think it means "doormat." It doesn't even mean the classic Canadian thing of apologizing if somebody steps on your foot. It may be a matter of a particular social situation. The quiet, ordinary folks who never make a big noise about themselves and never make the lifestyles of the rich and famous, except possibly as a chambermaid in the background, may be the meek.*

At that point, as you might guess, the sermon develops the beatitude "Blessed are the meek."

Here's a storytelling observation: the gold-rimmed glasses and the wispy mustache matter. A few small details are useful in preaching. The story of the prodigal son comes alive partly because of the detail that the young man was so hungry he would gladly have eaten the swill the pigs consumed, but no one gave a thing. The story of the good Samaritan gains more vigor because we know how much the Samaritan paid the innkeeper to care for the injured man. Note the specification: a few small details. Too many details clog the arteries of narrative like cholesterol. One might carry the image a little farther: our doctors tell us about good cholesterol and bad cholesterol. The right details are narrative good cholesterol. On a related note, details that connect the story to the social situation of the listeners may be particularly valuable. This story first appeared in a sermon preached in a Canadian church. Canadians laugh at themselves about their tendency to apologize too soon and too often. It doesn't matter if that is really the case if it is a matter of self-image. The detail in the negative description of what it means to be meek about apologizing if somebody steps on your foot helps the story to fit the situation.

Given above is a somewhat more polished version of a story than I would normally put in a database, largely because I have worked the material through into a sermon. But don't be "intimidated" by that minor degree of polish; all that matters is that the stories, anecdotes, and observations in your database be developed to the point that six months later, you will still know what you were talking about. Where that point is to be found, is up to you, the storyteller.

3

More on the Art of Storytelling

In the end, storytelling is an art that must be learned by observation and by practice. Storytellers are artisans, similar to potters. We learn by watching a master artisan and then by getting our fingers into the clay. Still, essential things can be said about the skills of storytelling, beginning with the skill of linking the story to the rest of the sermon or lesson—in other words, offering some clues to the purpose of the story in its setting.

Some may say that the strength of a story lies in its ambiguity and that interpretation may be at best unnecessary and at worst counterproductive. There is, after all, a famous definition of a parable, by the New Testament scholar, C. H. Dodd: "a simile or story drawn from life, the meaning of which is sufficiently uncertain to tease the mind into active thought."[1] Perhaps we ought not interpret a story lest it lose that capacity to tease the mind into active thought. It is true that some ambiguity is a good thing. Tying up every loose end in a story robs it of a potentially creative uncertainty that can stir reflection in the minds of our listeners. The question remains, however—active thought about what? A story, the meaning of which is so uncertain that it makes listeners think, what in heaven's name is that about? is not ambiguous. It leads the mind not into active thought but confusion. "There is no heaven but clarity, no hell but confusion," runs an old saying. Avoiding interpretation entirely runs the risk of hellish confusion. Moreover, sometimes the way a story is used is actually more interesting than the story itself. I have seen collections of stories told by famous preachers. Often I know how these stories are used in specific sermons. In the collections, however, they appear naked and

1. Dodd, *Parables of the Kingdom*, 5.

alone. They often lose what makes them wonderful without the links to the sermon as a whole. Interpretation matters.

If speaking and listening are working at all, the speaker is not the only one forming thoughts and ideas. Listeners are also engaged in their part, a silent part to be sure, of an interaction with the speaker. It may be that the worst thing that can happen to storytellers would be that their listeners simply tune out. The next worst thing is if a listener's response to a story includes some inner version of, Now what did that have to do with anything? Theoretically, a story can be so compelling that no interpretation may be necessary. The truth is, however, that most of our stories are not that good. Linking a story effectively to the flow of the sermon or lesson is normally vital. If a story is so obscure that extensive interpretation is necessary for listeners to understand why it is being told, it probably shouldn't be told at all, but many stories will need to be linked with some care to the rest of the sermon. This usually means that the preacher or teacher will need to interpret a story. Interpreting sensitively and, as in the temperature of Goldilocks's porridge, not too little, not too much, but just right, is a skill that can be practiced and developed.

I learned something more about all this from a woman named Emma . . .

What Emma Said

"I didn't listen to your sermon this morning, Stephen." So Emma said when she bustled up to me after church one Sunday morning. Most people say, "Thank you for the service," or "I enjoyed that sermon," or something of that order. That kind of response may be meaningless Pablum, but it does have the virtue of being easy to digest. Nothing like that ever came from Emma.

You need to know that Emma was not an easy woman to get along with. My first week in the congregation after being ordained, the elders suggested strongly that I visit two families who had declared that they intended to leave the church. It didn't work; both families left and never returned. Less than a week as a newly ordained minister and the church was down two families already! . . . The conversations with the soon-to-be departed were interesting, however. It turned out that, among other things, both families had been seriously at odds with Emma. At one home, they told me that Emma was possessed by a demon. In the other home, the verdict was that she was psychotic. When I got to know Emma, which did take some time, I came to realize that neither diagnosis was accurate. In fact, there was a good deal of love deep down in her heart. But it was well hidden by a near-terminal case of tactlessness.

Knowing all this, when Emma delivered her line, I wasn't at all surprised. I merely asked, "So, what did you do during the sermon?" In fact, I already knew of one thing she did every Sunday during the sermon. Emma was a soprano (the musical kind, not the gangster family, though sometimes it was hard to tell the difference) and invariably sat in the front row of the choir stalls, which gave her an excellent view of the congregation. Not to mention vice versa! Emma would write in the worship bulletin the name of everybody who was present at worship that day. That information was actually sometimes useful to me; the real problem came from the fact that she was nearsighted and had trouble recognizing people in the back pews. And, as we all know, the back pews are where a lot of the regulars in a church do like to sit. Emma would stare fixedly at the person or persons of uncertain identity and squint at them until she could bring their faces into focus. The chief consequence of all that was invariably to force her face into a ferocious grimace, a daunting mixture of concentration and myopia. It was even worse with guests or new worshipers. These people she couldn't recognize at all, no matter how long she stared, and she would frown at them until at last she gave it up as hopeless. Some of the newcomers would eventually tell me, if they stayed in our church, that they found it unnerving to have an otherwise normal-looking middle-aged woman staring at them as if they were likely to make off with the morning offering at gunpoint or to commit some equally heinous offense. This was a great help in church growth, of course.

But Emma didn't speak of any of that. She began, "You remember when you said thus and so?"

"Yes," I replied.

"Well, it made me think of my mother over in Beauton (a small city about an hour distant). She isn't getting any younger, and she seems to be getting more feeble every day. I can tell that she is lonely. My brother lives there too but he doesn't visit her very often. I thought about how I could ask him to visit her more often without making him so angry that he would visit her even less. I'm not very tactful, you know."

I bit the inside of my cheek. "Go on," I said.

"Then I figured out how I could make the time to visit her more often myself and finally I said a prayer for my mother."

I thought for a minute about what Emma had said to me and replied, "Emma, I don't know who else God spoke to this morning during the sermon but surely God spoke to you."

When I tell this story in class, I usually go on to speak about several things I learned that day. I learned, for one thing, that I am not in control of what people hear. Moreover, I tell the class, I think that most people listen to sermons or lessons the way Emma listened to me. If the sermon or lesson is a failure, they don't listen at all. But if it is actually working, they pay attention until they hear something that applies particularly to them, often in some way that the speaker could not possibly predict. At that point, listeners take off in their own directions, mulling over the matter until they reach some conclusion at least temporarily. This is the way I listen, and students seem to nod in agreement when I say this. It is the way they listen too, they generally respond. I am not speaking here of mere inattention, allowing our minds to wander to yesterday's game or what we will have for lunch. There is something very different from that, a theologically and spiritually creative mental wandering. Emma helped me to realize not only that this happens but that it is not a problem. It is very likely the way God speaks through a sermon or lesson.

In homiletics the unspoken goal, the *desideratum*, the perfect sermon, often seems to be an address that is so well crafted that everybody listens to the whole thing. Thanks to Emma, I no longer think that happens. Nor is it necessarily desirable. It might short-circuit the way God actually speaks to people. I also, think, however, that our listeners can come back into the sermon or lesson once their "Emma episode" is over. It may be that they are listening with a tendril of their mind, even while they are preoccupied with whatever it is that concerns them at the moment. Our task is not to create a sermon or lesson so compelling that every listener will listen to every word. It is rather to shape our words sufficiently clearly and with enough internal pointers and connectives that the wanderers can find where they are when they return. Among the most important of those pointers and connectives are the ones that link the stories we tell to the sermon or lesson as a whole. Emma and all our other listeners need those connectives. Those connectives usually come when we are interpreting our stories.

Appointment in Samarra

Here is a story I use in preaching class together with some potential interpretation that will link the story to the rest of a sermon. I do not know where the story comes from, though a 1934 novel has a title identical to the title of this section, "Appointment in Samarra." Somerset Maugham also told a version of this story but it is, I believe, considerably older than Maugham. This is the way I tell it, together with an interpretation.

Once upon a time, long, long ago, a man was walking towards the central market of old Baghdad. Suddenly, an acquaintance rushed towards him, obviously troubled, from the direction of the market.

"My good, friend," said the acquaintance. "Lend me your fastest horse, I beg you."

"Why should I do that, friend?" replied the man. "And why are you so distressed?"

"Because I met Death in the marketplace and Death made a threatening gesture towards me. But if I ride through the day and through the night on a swift horse, by tomorrow I will be in Samarra. And surely Death will not find me there."

So, upon reflection, the man lent his friend the horse, and he rode off furiously in the direction of Samarra. The man then resumed his interrupted journey to the marketplace. When he arrived, he discovered that his friend had been quite right. Death was indeed standing in the marketplace. Greatly daring, the man approached Death and said,

"Why did you make a threatening gesture towards my friend?" And Death replied, "It was not a threatening gesture but only a start of surprise. I did not expect to see him here for I have an appointment with him tomorrow in Samarra."

Perhaps it would be sufficient at this point to say, "We all have an appointment in Samarra or in . . ." (It works particularly well if you are in a community with a name beginning with the letter S.) But the Samarra Syndrome, the tendency to flee death or at least to do our very best to pretend that it is not there, is common enough in our society that we may want to say more. Perhaps we could go on to say something like the this:

We mock the Victorians for their prudish attitudes to sex. They were the ones who turned chicken "breast" into white meat and "thigh" into dark meat. After all, no hostess would have wanted to turn to a gentleman caller and say, "Care for a little leg?" The female leg was apparently a particular source of stimulation to the Victorian imagination. It is said that some hostesses even put trousers on the curving legs of their pianos or their dining tables lest those Victorian gentlemen in their waistcoats and mutton chop whiskers should grow overheated in their imaginations. In my opinion anyone who can look at a piano leg and think "sex" has a really dirty mind. But apparently so it was in Victorian times.

The truth is, however, that we can, with some difficulty, avoid sex in our lives. But we scoffing contemporaries attempt something much more difficult—in fact impossible according to reliable accounts. We try to avoid death or, since in our heart of hearts we know that we cannot do this, we pretend that death does not exist. When we do not want to speak directly about a subject, when it embarrasses or troubles us, we employ euphemisms. There are many euphemisms for sex and just as many for death. In a traditional *obituary* in my part of the world (not in a *death notice*; that would be crude) no verb appears at the beginning. The obituary simply commences, "Suddenly" or "After a long illness" or "Despite a brave struggle." "Suddenly" what? Did the person get tired of the winters up here and move to Florida? We all know, of course, what has happened, but we do not say it aloud. That which we know but do not wish to say aloud is that which we fear. We fear death but we cannot avoid it. We all have an appointment in Samarra or elsewhere.

As we have seen, *stories tell a truth or, indeed, several truths.* They communicate in a way that cannot quite be equaled in any other form. In this book I cannot answer Pilate's question, "What is truth?" For my purposes here, a truth is whatever of lasting value the speaker hopes to convey by telling a story. If storytellers have nothing identifiable they wish to convey, their lack of expectations will likely be fulfilled. Now, the question arises: should we interpret a story? Or should we simply "trust the story" and leave it to make its point? It is true that we ought not overinterpret the stories we tell. Sometimes a long interpretation robs a story of its power. You want to protest to the overinterpreting storyteller, "I get it already!" It is also normally a mistake to offer an interpretation *before* telling a story. Imagine a preacher introducing "Appointment in Samarra."

"I would like to tell you a story that illustrates the great Christian truth that death is inevitable and that it always foolish to try to avoid it or pretend that it doesn't exist." To do so is equivalent to writing a detective story that begins: "I would like to tell you a detective story in which a man is murdered by his faithless wife and his embezzling business partner." Neither approach is a good idea. We don't want to find out "whodunit" until the last page or two of our mystery novel, and we usually don't want to hear what a story is about until very near its conclusion.

Many stories, especially those more complex than "Appointment in Samarra" convey more than one truth. It is quite possible to move from the story in several rather different directions. In fact, I have sometimes used with my preaching students a class exercise in which I supply a story and ask what scriptural text or theme the students would link it to. The class invariably can think of half a dozen or more different biblical themes and texts that could be enriched by the story. There is nothing wrong in a sermon or a lesson with identifying beforehand the particular path to be taken once a story is over. If we do, the Emmas in our church may actually be able to follow us.

Moreover a good story evokes reflections, ideas, and concepts. Even when a story has a very clear point, the story can be effectively extended to give voice to the thoughts that the story engenders in you the speaker. You will notice that I expanded and interpreted "Appointment in Samarra" by reflecting on our society's reluctance to face death. Overinterpretation is a mistake in storytelling, but this does not mean that interpretation itself is wrong. What is the difference between interpretation and over-interpretation? It's a matter of taste. But too little is probably better than too much.

ON SPLITTING STORIES

One effective storytelling technique links a story not just to one moment in a sermon or lesson but rather to part of the sermon or lesson's flow. This technique is to split a story—that is, tell its beginning at one point and apparently to bring it to a conclusion but then to introduce its actual conclusion sometime later. You might call this the Paul Harvey technique. Harvey was a radio personality who specialized in short, human interest yarns. His stories invariably paused in the middle, usually allowing time for an advertisement. When the ad concluded, he would say, "And now for the rest of the story!" The "rest of the story" invariably added some fascinating little twist to the tale. I have already used this technique in the Trail casserole story. Here is another example. It requires some understanding of the context in which I told it.

One of the problems of much of our preaching and teaching, perhaps particularly with respect to the First Testament, is that we personalize, individualize, and thus trivialize what is happening in the text. Thus, for example, sermons on the dry bones of Ezek 37 often become reflections on times of spiritual dryness in our lives when we just can't pray very effectively and life seems empty to us. I do not mean to diminish the pain of such experiences, especially if clinical depression is a factor in the dryness. But the exiles in Babylon to whom Ezekiel was speaking had experienced something far worse than spiritual dryness or a temporary incapacity for prayer. Life had completely fallen apart for them. The institutions of their culture, which had given them meaning and purpose, had disappeared or disintegrated. They had seen friends, neighbors, and family members slaughtered. They themselves had been dragged to refugee camps far from their homes, and, as far as they could tell, had no hope of return. They held out no hope for anything. Compared to all this, our spiritual discomforts are often first world problems. A Syrian refugee fleeing ISIS might be able to tell us what a valley of dry bones feels like. For a person sitting in a pew in a church formed by Western culture, it is more difficult. I needed for this sermon something more serious than spiritual dryness. I thought of my friend Jacques.

Jacques

Jacques was part of a group of Christians (of which I also was a member) from different parts of the world. We met once a year, if possible. It was not always possible for Jacques. He was the minister in one of the world's notorious hellholes, in a city and country where everyday chaos was always about to descend into outright civil war. One year, for example, he had to be rowed at night to a freighter offshore to get to a city in another country in order to catch a flight to attend our meeting. He was normally reasonably cheerful, however.

That was the case until the country actually slid into another bout of civil war. The next time we met, he told me what had happened. The violence came on very suddenly, His church, in the heart of the capital city, also ran a large school, he explained . Fighting erupted so quickly that they could not get all the children safely to their families or to refuges in the hills surrounding the city. He and his wife were left in the church as shells were bursting around them. There were two hundred children, he said, with no medicine and very little food or water. He and his wife were totally responsible for the care of the children.

Jacques was a big, strong, healthy young man, and his wife, whose photo I had seen, was a beautiful woman, the picture of loveliness. They had been a couple bursting with life. But Jacques shuddered as he told me, "We *aren't going to have children. We have decided that we cannot bring children into a world like this."*

When life is so bad that it seems wrong even to bring new life into the world, then the world is a valley of dry bones.

I ended the story, as it seemed, at this point, and proceeded to say the things one normally says about a text like Ezek 37. I described the situation of the exiles in Babylon, and I spoke of the command to the prophet to preach the word in these dreadful circumstances. I testified to the new hope that the word of God can bring in that valley of dry bones. Then, very near the end of the sermon, I said this:

I remember the last time I saw Jacques. His country had been blessed with relative peace and security. He took me aside and showed me a photo of two little girls—girls as beautiful as their mother—two girls, his daughters.

There is always hope when God is at work.

THE RIGHT LEVEL OF DETAIL

Getting the level of detail right in a story is both helpful and challenging. In the first place, the details often make a story interesting. Consider this news item from my longtime home city of Vancouver, British Columbia:

Goldilocks's Revenge

Vancouver backs onto genuine wilderness. In fact, all too often, a lost skier, hiker or climber has an accident and dies in the wilderness. And sometimes the wilderness makes its way into the city. A year or two ago, a woman arrived at her home in North Vancouver (a community which lies up against the forests of the North Shore mountains.) She went into the house and realized, to her horror, that a bear was in her kitchen."

That is, at best, a mildly interesting little anecdote. It becomes much more interesting when a detail is added.

"The bear was finishing off her leftover porridge."

I then add a sentence: "It is not known whether the porridge was too hot, too cold or just right."

The detail about the porridge makes the story.

That was a story from the local newspaper. What do we do when we are creating something that does not come to us ready-made? What do we do when rather we are attempting to speak or write of something from our own experience? In the first chapter of this book I attempted to distinguish between an observation and a story. Perhaps we can turn an example of an observation into a story by adding a few details.

Picture a set of lights controlled by a motion sensor. Sometimes you have to take a step before the lights will shine.

Though it is true, that observation is not very interesting. A few more details will help.

Picture turning a corner into a corridor of, say, an inexpensive hotel. You do not know the building, and it appears the owners have decided to save money and electricity by installing motion sensors in the hallways. Perhaps your room is down that dark hallway, perhaps not. The only thing you can see of the way ahead is that you cannot see at all. You have to step forward into the darkness in the trust that, if you take the step, the light will shine.

That remains an observation at this point, but it is somewhat more interesting because of the extra details. In order to change this observation into a story we must change the material from a generalized observation about an often repeated phenomenon to an account of a specific event. That will mean that we must create a specific character who is faced with the dark corridor. This anecdote comes from an experience of my own, so I will make it a first-person account. Turning it into a story will probably also mean adding yet a few more details:

The other day I checked into an inexpensive hotel in the southern French city of Nîmes.

That happens to be the case, but perhaps it would be better to leave out of this story the location of the hotel. For one thing, if I include it, the story could sound like an indirect boast, as if I were actually trying to communicate not the gospel but what a cosmopolitan traveler I am. The listener reactions may not be as negative as that, but it might be that some listeners have also been to Nîmes. Instead of listening to whatever I have to say next, they will follow the path that Emma followed. Their version of the Emma phenomenon might be to think, I wonder if Stephen visited the Roman aqueduct there. It was spectacular! . . . I'll never forget that aqueduct. I must ask Stephen about that after the service.

So on balance, it would be best to leave out of this story the hotel's location. It also happens that my wife was with me, but that detail does not actually affect the flow of the story, so I left it out. It would be easy, however, to add "my wife and I," or, if the listeners know her, "Patty and I."

The other day I checked into an inexpensive hotel. The owners of the hotel had obviously decided to save money and electricity by installing motion sensors in the hallways. Room key in hand, I climbed the main stair of the aging hotel and turned towards an upper corridor down which, I hoped, my room could be found. It was very dark indeed in that empty corridor. The only thing you could see of the way ahead was that you could not see at all. You had to step forward into the darkness in the trust that, if you take the step, the light will shine.

This has become a rather skeletal story with a character, myself in this case, and a conundrum, which nears the status of a plot. Something has happened and something further, and more important may happen. Will I step forward into the darkness, in the trust that light will be there? If I do not step forward, what will happen? Will I stand there all night, room key in hand, or at least until some more intrepid fellow guest steps by and activates the motion sensor? It would be possible to resolve the matter. *I stepped forward and the light shone in the darkness.*

But good storytelling is often a matter of instinct, and my instinct is that it would be better to let the listeners fill in the conclusion themselves. This is scarcely the equivalent of the cliff-hanger in the end-of-season episode of a TV drama, but perhaps what little tension is present in the story ought to be left intact.

Some degree of interpretation is useful here, however. Perhaps it could be as simple as, *"In the life of faith, sometimes we have to step into the darkness before we can see the light."*

In this case, I would probably be speaking about the existential leap of faith, stepping forward when we are uncertain of the way ahead. If I did add the phrase, "And the light shone in the darkness," I would be declaring the promise of the gospel that the light of Christ's presence does shine in the darkness, and if we step forward in faith, we will perceive his light. That phrase would even serve to link the story to a specific biblical text, John 1:5, "And the light shines in the darkness and the darkness did not overcome it." (Or "understood it," as the Greek could also be rendered, which is something worth thinking about.) Both the details in the story and the act of interpretation can make statements of surprising weight.

The details we elect to include can also change the direction of the story. Here is another detail, also factually accurate, as it happens, that could be added to the story. *But ahead of me was the concierge, leading the way. It is easier to step into the darkness if you are not alone, if you are with someone who knows the way.*

But note that adding this factual detail may alter substantially the direction of the story. Now the story is not primarily about an existential step of faith in the darkness in the hope of encountering the light of Christ. It could be about the role of mentors in the Christian faith who have walked the dark corridors before us. It could, in fact, be about the church, the fellowship of those who have gone before us and know the way.

Another possibility would be to emphasize in the story not he present darkness but the ultimate destination. *Down the corridor, I knew, was home for the night and rest at last.* If this emphasis is chosen, it would be good to prepare for this turn early in the story by adding a few of those details that often matter so much. *But after a long and very tiring day, when there was precious little fuel left in the tank and every little thing thing seemed a burden and an imposition, I checked into an inexpensive hotel.* A different interpretation would then be needed. *Rest at the last. It's there when we step into the darkness.* There might well be a preaching or teaching situation in which such a word would bring comfort.

The combination of details in the story itself and the words of interpretation which follow it signal to the listener which direction the sermon or lesson is going with the story. Most listeners need this, but none more than the Emma of the day, if she is stepping back into the sermon or lesson. The effective storyteller needs to learn how to do both and, quite probably, both in tandem.

One more thing can be said in this connection. Most stories offer so many directions that whatever database we create to keep track of our stories ought not to be excessively precise about how we intend to use them.

If you write out a story at any level of detail, punctuate the story the way you would speak or read it. This will probably mean that you will use more commas than a grammatical purist would advise. These commas represent the frequent small pauses that make oral communication successful. They serve as a recognition from near the beginning of the process that the end result of a story is to speak or read aloud effectively.

THE USE OF HUMOR

Little is more tedious or less funny than reading about humor. Writing about it may be even worse. But the subject is so closely related to storytelling that we cannot simply give it a miss.

When we think of humor, most of us think first of jokes. That may be a mistake. Many years ago, a minister sought me out for a private consultation on his preaching. He wasn't, as far as I know, in any trouble in his congregation. He had simply come to the conclusion that there was room for improvement in his preaching. More clergy should do this. I do not mean that they should come to me for a consultation, of course. I mean they should seek someone out from time to time to provide a dispassionate and even, one hopes, an expert evaluation of some sample sermons. Here is an aside about clergy who are, in fact, in trouble in their situations, of which there are many: Church judicatories regularly require and even help pay for psychological assessments of clergy in difficulties in their parishes or congregations. Sometimes, however, the problem, or one the problems, is not that the clergy are unstable or disturbed; it is that they are terrible preachers. The judicatory and struggling pastors or priests would sometimes find a better return on investment in a consultation on the quality of their preaching. But that too is another story.

This particular preacher brought me a half dozen or so sample sermons, which I read and listened to with interest. The most immediately striking feature of the sermons was that he began each one with a joke. I asked the minister why he did that.

"So that they will like me," he replied plaintively.

I think, or perhaps I hope, that I kept a generally expressionless face when he said that. It all seemed a little sad and even a little desperate. Notwithstanding the role of ethos, or the perceived character of the speaker in the effectiveness of persuasion, our job is not to make people like us. It is to help people to love Jesus. Moreover, it is unlikely that telling a joke at the beginning of every Sunday's sermon will suffice to make people like us. They like or dislike us for a wide variety of reasons, most of which have little to do with jokes. Are you courteous in speaking and acting? Are you generous with your time and attention? Did you sit with a widow when her husband was dying? Those things matter much more than jokes.

Jokes, as such, are actually problematic in preaching and teaching.

The Stutter

Years ago as a very young man, I was helping with a camping program for a group of teenage boys. We pitched our tents in the bush, but on Sunday we piled all the boys into a van and drove them to church in a nearby town. Our boys didn't actually resent having to go to church. Anything to get away from the tents . . . and the bugs. Those were the days when even teenage boys were expected to wear jackets, ties, and polished shoes to church and to behave with decorum. It only seemed fair to us to warn the preacher that he would have a significant addition to the congregation that would not fit the mold. Perhaps we even hoped the preacher might adjust his sermon to communicate with our group of boys. Perhaps, knowing that there would be a group of teenage boys in the congregation, the minister thought that telling a joke would be a good idea.

I still remember the joke all these years later:

Once there was a veteran instructor in the army's paratrooper school. In a particular group of his trainees was one candidate who had a terrible stutter, made even worse by his evident anxiety about his approaching first jump. The instructor was used to this kind of prejump anxiety and he made light of it with the young man.

"You have nothing to worry about," he said. "Just jump out of the plane, count to three and pull the cord. You'll be just fine. In fact, to show you how easy it is, I'll jump first!"

The day of the first jump arrived. True to his word, the instructor jumped first. "One, Two, Three," he counted and pulled the cord. The chute opened and the instructor began to float gently towards earth.

Then a body flashed by, hurtling earthwards, and the instructor heard, "T-t-t-t-t-twooo!"

Perhaps the joke was better than a children's story about the good things Hitler did, but that does not make telling it a good idea. In the first place, I remember the joke all these years later but do not have the faintest idea what the sermon was about. Admittedly, that may happen even with good jokes. In fact, it is more likely to happen with a good joke! This joke, however, is less than kind to people with a speech impediment such as a stutter. As it happens, I sometimes struggle with a slight impediment, especially if I am tired. It's not usually so much a full stutter as a hesitation, an inability to get the next sound out. I have almost entirely overcome it through the years, but the memory of my irritation is still there. I didn't like the joke, and I was grateful that none of our boys had a stutter. I am quite sure the minister did not mean to offend anyone. One common use of humor is to wound, and this was clearly not his intention. Whatever his intentions may have been, the joke didn't work.

In one set of circumstances that minister could have turned the joke around. It could work if the jokester himself had a stutter. "Did I ever tell you about my time in the paratroops?" the joke teller could begin. He would then recast the story in the first-person singular and go hurtling past the instructor. Perhaps the joke could then end,

Well, I got to "three" in time, barely, and the chute opened, bringing me safely to the ground. The instructor approached me, put his arm around my shoulders and said, "Son, have you ever considered a career in the infantry?"

I do not know how that version works for you, but to me it is markedly less offensive. The reason it is less offensive points to a most important principle with respect to the use of humor: Only tell jokes, especially ones that have a tinge of mockery, about yourself or your own group. And the second commandment is like unto it; do not tell jokes that mock the challenges, weaknesses, or infirmities of others.

I could count the number of actual jokes I have ever told in sermons on the fingers of one hand and have a finger or two left over. Here, however, is one of the jokes that I have told. It appears in a sermon called, "Fuhgedaboudid!"—based on one of the two passages in the Bible that make forgetting, rather than remembering, a good thing: "This one thing I do, forgetting what is behind and straining forward to what lies ahead, I press on toward the goal for the prize of the heavenly call of God in Christ Jesus" (Phil 3:13–14). (The other text is Isa 43:18: "Do not remember the former things, / or consider the things of old.") In the course of the sermon, I say that in church we are far too prone to hang on to the wrong kind of memories.

How many Presbyterians does it take to change a light bulb?

It takes ten, one to change the light bulb and the other nine to say how much nicer the old bulb was.

Sometimes you just want to say, "Fuhgedaboudid!"

It is worth telling that joke because it has a ring of truth. But not everybody should tell that joke. Earlier in the third chapter of Philippians, where the scriptural basis for this sermon is found, Paul tells his hearers and readers that when it comes to being Jewish, he is the real thing. In the same manner, when it comes to being Presbyterian, I too am very definitely the real thing. I can tell that joke because I am Presbyterian. Of course, that joke is but one of a large family of light bulb jokes. I think the one about how many Unitarians it takes to change a light bulb is just as funny. But I ought not tell it from the pulpit, or in this book; it belongs to the Unitarians.

In this case people will indeed remember the light bulb joke, but unlike listeners to the joke about the stuttering paratrooper, hearers will also be able to recall the point I was trying to make: some things need to be left behind and forgotten. The sermon under discussion here is useful for many different congregations. As a result, I have used it a number of times on special occasions as a guest preacher, on anniversary Sundays, for example. As far as I can tell from postsermon, over-the-coffee-cup conversations, people do understand why I tell the joke.

Humor can be useful in sermons and lessons, and when it serves to delight rather than to wound, is a good thing in itself; but humor is not confined to jokes. Some preachers and other speakers are as funny as the best stand-up comedians without ever telling jokes. Their humor comes from the use of colorful language, from the apprehension of the incongruous, and from the wry observation of reality.

For example, in the sermon "Fuhgedaboudid," I wanted to set the Letter to the Philippians in its context. Paul is in jail, and he is writing to the Philippians to say thank you for their support (probably a gift of money). I tried, therefore, to picture the jail cell for the listeners. There is Paul pacing back and forth, one step, two steps, three steps, turn. One step, two steps, three steps turn. Outside the door is a Roman guard— "Looks like John Wayne, but not so feminine." It is not my own line. I heard it somewhere and filed it away until an appropriate time. Good lines are like stories; we come upon them more than we create them. People generally laugh at that line at least as heartily as at the light bulb joke. Do they laugh because the language is colorful enough for them to picture John Wayne in a Roman centurion's costume? Perhaps because the line attaches the adjective *feminine* to John Wayne—an attachment so contrary to any kind of perceived reality about the great actor that it is incongruous. One of the problems with humor, by the way, is that some people will not get it. I was once scolded at the church door after preaching "Fuhgedaboudid" by a gentleman who thought I was mocking the Duke. Humor is not, of course, all that can be misunderstood. If we refrain from speaking because someone may misunderstand, we will all be mutes.

Humor creates delight in listeners, and delight is a worthwhile end in itself. But humor can also be the key to a door in the human heart through which matters of great seriousness may pass in their turn. One master of using humor as an entrée into serious matters was the late Fred Craddock, a preacher who employed humor without telling jokes. Craddock has the remarkable gift of offering such wry observations of our common humanity that we laugh and laugh again. We laugh, in fact, until Craddock changes the angle of approach but a quarter turn and we are, it may well be, closer to tears. One of his most famous sermons was "When the Roll Is Called Down Here," on the list of names—the roll call, as it were—at the end of the Letter to the Romans. Craddock tells of being called to jury duty in superior court, in DeKalb County, Georgia, and listening to the clerk of the court call the roll. Craddock's use of language is so clever and his observations of human nature so perceptive that we laugh heartily. We laugh until the woman sitting next to Craddock tells him she was raised in Germany during the war.

"Well you were just a little child when all of that happened, years ago."

"I was ten years old. I visited Grandmother, who lived about four miles from Buchenwald. I smelled the odor."

We aren't laughing anymore, but we are ready to believe that somewhere behind even a list of names there can be pathos. We are more ready to sense the pathos precisely because we have been laughing. We might want to protect ourselves from the tragedy behind a childhood memory of the Holocaust, but we have lowered our defenses because of our laughter. Humor prepares the way for the serious insight. That insight, as it turns out, is necessary for the rest of the sermon.

Humor is meant to be experienced rather than written about. Fortunately, Craddock's great sermon can still be experienced on YouTube.[2]

To return to "Fuhgedaboudid," the sense that Paul is trapped is vital for the remainder of the sermon. He is trapped, not just by the prison walls, or by the guards, but by the wrong kind of memories. One step, two steps, three steps, turn. As long as he is thinking about his past, his status, his suffering, he is in chains. But when Paul begins to think of Jesus, something wonderful happens. The language changes. Paul uses imagery associated with the Olympics and other games of the ancient world. One step, two steps, three steps and the gold medal. And if you are ahead in a race, what is the one thing you never do? You never look behind you! Or, in other words, "Fuhgedaboudid." The humor is one small detail that prepares for a vital and very serious turn in the sermon. To prepare for something serious, that is the real reason for using humor in a sermon or lesson.

One real option for many of us, however, is simply not to use humour. The truth is that some people just are not funny. If you recall the movie *Good Morning, Vietnam!* think of Lieutenant Hauk and his imaginary radio sidekick, Frenchy. "In my heart I know I'm funny!"[3] He isn't, and because of the incongruity between his self-perception and his actual personality (not to mention the echo of the Barry Goldwater presidential campaign slogan), the line is one of the funniest moments in the movie. One person can deliver a line and the audience howls. The next person says almost the same words and the listeners cringe. If you are not funny, don't try to be what you are not. It may well be that we value humor

---

2. See Craddock, "When the Roll Is Called Down Here."
3. See this clip of Lieutenant Hauk: https://youtu.be/u7Ty3fggeBA/.

too highly in public speaking and in society in general. There is nothing wrong or shameful about not being funny. Preachers or teachers who know or even just suspect that they are not funny should just forget about it. It may also be the case that, if they lack the self-knowledge to realize they are not funny, they have a bigger problem than lacking the gift of humor.

WHAT DOES MATTER IN PREACHING

Humor is useful in preaching and teaching, but it is not even within hailing distance of being the most important gift of the preacher and teacher. Cardinal John Henry Newman, the high church Anglican who became a Roman Catholic cardinal of the Victorian era, himself a great preacher, identified the one thing needful in a preacher as "earnestness."[4] Though the word may sound as Victorian as Newman himself, it is a useful thought. The word *earnestness* conveys seriousness. People must be able to perceive that we are dead serious about what we are saying. They must know that we think what we are trying to communicate is of immense weight, and that it matters that they accept what we have to say. Earnestness is not enough, however. Most of us know preachers and teachers who are so earnest that they ooze sincerity from every pore but are as dull as a whole bag of doorknobs. When they are speaking, we would like simply to slip out the back door. Well-intentioned but dull may have been good enough to get by in times past, but that is not so in the present state of the church.

The Welsh have a wonderful word for what many value in good speaking, *hwyl*. (It is pronounced more or less as "who eel," but in one syllable.) As a mere tongue-tied Anglo-Saxon, I hesitate to speak about Welsh, but I understand the word has a wide range of meanings. Perhaps the classic use of the word, however applies to preachers who from time to time are so taken up with the magnificence of the gospel that their words take flight. *Hwyl* is not shouting or pulpit histrionics. Rather, it is an audible and visible earnestness combined with passion. It is not an attainment but a gift.

Another way of saying all this is that the preacher must be claimed by the gospel and the claim must show.

---

4. See Burghardt, *Preaching: The Art and the Craft.*

TALKING ABOUT OURSELVES

The Preacher's Daughter-in-Law

I remember the time our family was visiting a large American city. On Sunday morning we attended a first-steeple type church where a retired but well-known preacher was filling in. I thought the sermon was excellent. Sometimes later, back in Canada, I was talking with a friend who had studied in that city, knew it well, and retained a deep affection for it. I mentioned where we had worshiped, knowing that my friend held this deep affection. He would certainly be familiar with the church and might even know of the preacher I had heard. As it turned out, he had indeed heard the preacher many times.

"Did he begin with a story about himself or his family?" my friend asked, in a surprisingly jaded tone. The preacher had indeed done just that. He had begun the sermon with a lengthy story about his brilliant and charming daughter-in-law.

"Yes," I replied.

My friend shrugged. "He always does."

It is not the case that we should never tell stories about our families. Anyone who has read this book to this point will realize that it would be hypocritical of me to suggest that, even for a moment. But it is not all we should do. Preachers who never change their style are like baseball pitchers who never throw a changeup. Sooner or later they will be hit hard. For readers who do not know baseball, a changeup is, as the name suggests, a change-of-pace pitch. It looks like a pitcher's normal fastball but comes in to the plate at a considerably slower rate. Batters have all but completed their swing before the ball even arrives at the plate. Good hitters will eventually get the timing of even an excellent fastball if the pitcher never changes pace. Preachers and teachers need to change pace from time to time also. Variety is vital, both in the way we speak and in the way we use our stories.

The problem is especially acute for preachers and teachers when we tell stories about ourselves and our own families. There was a time in living memory when many preachers were reluctant to tell stories about themselves. If they did so, they might begin by saying, "if you will forgive a personal illustration." That does not often happen anymore, but the matter is more serious than merely being out of homiletical fashion. At least one teacher of preaching of a more recent vintage, David Buttrick, has strongly discouraged first-person-singular references, however, arguing that they introduce a split in consciousness in our listeners.[5] Listeners' minds are divided between whatever they think of us as a result of hearing the story and whatever it is the speaker is trying to convey. Furthermore, stories of any kind have the capacity to overshadow their surrounding material.[6] This problem must be taken seriously. Preachers and teachers need to read, mark, learn and inwardly digest the famous first line of *The Purpose Driven Life*: "It's not about you."[7]

Saying that stories may overshadow their surrounding material is another way of saying stories are powerful or, in other words, that they work. Turning away from storytelling because stories are powerful and they work seems a little peculiar. "Luke, you shouldn't have put in that story about the Samaritan. Who is going to remember the rest of the chapter?" When most of us think of powerful preachers and teachers (as I think of Fred Craddock, for example), those persons are for many of us likely to be consummately skilled storytellers. The key to a right use of stories is that the stories must pull in the same direction as the surrounding material. That means, as I noted above, that we need some means of retaining stories until they can be used at the right time, in the right place, in the right context.

This still leaves the problem of stories about ourselves and our own families. The difficulty is that many of our best and most compelling stories are indeed about our own experiences. Anecdotes that we glean from the internet or from printed collections of stories often seem dry and lifeless by comparison. But *difficulty* may not be entirely the right word in this connection. In the end, sermons and lessons in this Christianity business must have an element of testimony about them. We must be able to bear witness to what God has done for us. We must be able to say, "A wandering Aramaean was my father," or "I once was lost and now am

5. See Buttrick, *Homiletic*.

6. There is also a theological conundrum here, particularly for those influenced by Karl Barth. Does an excessive reliance on stories, particularly our own stories, convey the impression that the starting point for hearing God's word is reflection on our own experience? For the significance of Barth's theology for preaching see Willimon, *Conversations with Barth on Preaching*. Willimon himself definitely qualifies as a consummately skilled storyteller.

7. Warren, *The Purpose-Driven Life*, 1.

found." That will mean telling our stories. Over the years, I have come to this conclusion: stories about ourselves and our families are like strong medicine. They are powerful stuff, and it is both easiest and most dangerous to overdose on strong medicine. We need to be careful in using them.

One way to handle this problem is to employ what might be called the 2 Corinthians tactic. In the concluding section of that letter Paul is under attack, and he does speak about himself extensively in 2 Cor 11:16-29. There he refers to his many sufferings for the gospel. We wish we knew more about them because many of these have to do with events that are not recorded in the Acts of the Apostles. Sadly, they are stories that can no longer be told. When he reaches the high point, as it were, of his argument, however, he does not speak directly of himself: " I know a person in Christ who fourteen years ago was caught up to the third heaven—whether in the body or out of the body I do not know; God knows. And I know that such a person, whether in the body or out of the body I do not know; God knows, was caught up into Paradise and heard things that are not to be told, that no mortal is permitted to repeat." (2 Cor 12:2–4). Most scholars agree that Paul is talking about himself here. He himself is the person caught up into heaven. The tactic, then, is to tell a story about ourselves in the third person. This may maintain the vigor and freshness of the personal story but may not suffer from the problem of the potential split in consciousness that can attend a first-person story. It may not work, however. When I have used this technique, someone always seems to approach me after the sermon and asks, "Was that story really about you?" That may be evidence of a split in consciousness in itself. Still, the 2 Corinthians tactic is probably still worth trying.

When we tell stories about ourselves and our families, we do inevitably communicate something about ourselves. There is a difficult balancing point here. Stories about our successes and accomplishments sound like and probably are boasting, "Did I tell you about the time in high school when I sank both ends of a one-and-one to win the city basketball championship?" Self-deprecating stories work better and are certainly more likely to be funny, if that is our aim.

The Coolness Factor

Shortly after we moved to Vancouver there was a meeting of our presbytery, the local council of clergy and representative elders. The presbytery owns a camp, and the chair of the camp committee, a middle-aged lady named

Maggie, was presenting a report on the state of the camp to the presbytery. Though I had just arrived in the area, Maggie and I had known each other at least slightly for a number of years. Her presentation was excellent and culminated in an appeal to the ministers of the presbytery to give up a week of their vacation to serve as volunteer chaplains for campers in various age groups.

As I drove home, I thought about the speech. I said to myself, "You should do that. Probably the youth camp would be the best choice. After all, these are the kids who might consider becoming ministers, and even if they don't do that, they want to live in our residence if they come to the University of British Columbia. You ought to get to know them."

The next day, I phoned Maggie. "That was an excellent presentation last night. It got me thinking," I told her.

"Thanks," she said.

"In fact, it made me think that I should volunteer as a chaplain. I would like to volunteer for the youth camp."

Dead silence.

"Well, Stephen," Maggie finally replied, "I think we were hoping for someone with a higher coolness factor than you!"

I never did get to be a camp chaplain. The story has turned out to be useful over the years, however. When I have been invited to speak to gatherings of youth—it does happen occasionally, usually with people who do not know me well—I introduce myself with this story. The young people laugh, relax, and seem to listen better to the more serious parts of my address. That would be fine if it were the only such story I tell. The potential problem, however, is that when I look at the stories I tell about myself over the years, they tend to be at least as self-deprecating as this one. I ask myself sometimes if I constantly present myself as an awkward klutz, as a lousy dancer, as clueless with women and, of course, as the possessor of a terminally low coolness factor. Those things may be true, but they are not the whole truth about me. Do I misrepresent myself by the selection of stories I tell?

The key here for all of us may be asking the question, what do these stories, taken as a whole, communicate about me? And, more important, is communicating something about me my main task today?

4

Is That Story True?
Ethics and Storytelling

Ethical storytelling is all about telling the truth. Many people think, not entirely wrongly, that what is true is factual, and vice versa. But it ain't necessarily so. Think, to take an obvious example, of the parable of the Good Samaritan. It would not have appeared in the first-century equivalent of the *Jerusalem Daily Post*, had there been one at the time, because Jesus made up the story. He told the story, however, to convey something that, though not factual, is profoundly true. That something is often called a point, though that language has been challenged in more recent years. Without committing to any particular scholarly position about the way parables work, let us use the word *point* as a convenient shorthand for whatever it is that parables or other stories do convey. The point of the Good Samaritan parable is true. On the other hand, much of what appears in our daily newspaper (or increasingly in our online news sources), is factually accurate, or one so hopes at least. But a day later the factual report is yesterday's electrons or, for the more old-fashioned among us, is lining the bottom of the bird cage. The parable, though it is a made-up tale, teaches us something so profoundly true that it is worth living our lives by. The other is merely factual. All this is to say, then, that the criterion for truth in storytelling is whether the story conveys something that is worth living by, or in short, something true.

None of this should be taken to mean that the factual is unimportant. I remain unrepentantly convinced that our faith is in vain if there are not some hard core historical facts associated with the stories of Israel and of Jesus recounted in the Bible. We can debate which facts at are essential at some other point. I am also convinced that the best true stories often rest on a bedrock of fact. I am further convinced, and this is more relevant to this chapter, that it is unethical to represent as factual that which is not. To do so is to speak something untrue.

You will have to decide for yourself, in light of your tradition, what constitutes that "something true" in our storytelling. For the purposes of this book, indeed, for the purposes of my own storytelling, I use a version of what the great thinker, Augustine of Hippo, said in the first Christian textbook on preaching and biblical interpretation, *De Doctrina Christiana.* Augustine was faced with the problem of what to do with biblical texts that seem to advocate violence or to picture God as violent and cruel if read literally. In such cases, an interpreter was justified, he argued, in adopting a spiritual rather than a literal reading of the text. So, for example, the conquest and slaughter of the Canaanites by the children of Israel could be read as a conquest of our own evil tendencies. (This is not radically different from the way moderate Muslims interpret the concept of *jihad,* by the way.) When dealing with a text that was ambiguous or even unambiguously violent, Augustine wrote, "you should refer it to the rule of faith which you have received from the plainer parts of Scripture and from the authority of the church."[1]

More specifically, Augustine consistently emphasized the primacy of love. Right interpretation must be for the "nourishment of charity."[2] "All such stories . . . are not only to be interpreted literally as historical accounts but also to be taken figuratively as prophetic in some way, pointing to that end of the love of God or of neighbor or of both."[3] The preacher should always seek that reading of Scripture that increases the love of God or love of the neighbor, or both. That criterion or "rule of faith," still works for the contemporary storyteller in my view. To this we might add an emphasis from Martin Luther. Luther argued that a correct reading of Scripture is *was treibt Christum,* "that which pushes Christ."[4] A story is "true" and worth using if it leads to greater love of God or of the neighbor, or both. And a story should serve to "push Christ."

A key part of ethical storytelling is to have the equivalent of what Augustine called the "rule of faith," that is an interpretive principle that allows you to make responsible selection and use of all those stories out

1. Augustine of Hippo, *De Doctrina Christiana,* as translated in Lischer, *The Company of Preachers,* 170.

2. Augustine of Hippo, *De Doctrina Christiana* (ibid., 174).

3. Augustine of Hippo, *De Doctrina Christiana* (ibid.,175).

4. Olson, *The Mosaic of Christian Belief,* 66.

there in the service of some particular end. The question then is whether that interpretive principle is shaped by the gospel.

This is not to say that storytellers may only tell edifying tales that radiate peace, harmony and "niceness," as if they were scriptwriters for a *Care Bears* episode. Stories with some of the grit of life in them are more than useful. They are the roughage of spiritual nutrition. A preacher or teacher may sometimes rightly use stories that neither lead directly to greater love nor push Christ. Some great preachers and teachers of preaching adopt a "law-gospel" structure in their preaching. Law can be understood as all that distances us from the love of God. I have theological difficulties with using the word *law* in this manner, but let it stand for a moment. Such sermons have a "good news-bad news" or "down-up" structure. The first move of the sermon is a presentation of human life as it is lived distant from God. The second half presents the good news of an abundant life that is God's will for all creation. It is possible to use a story powerfully to image that first movement, and it is unlikely that such a story will directly nourish charity. It may, however, prepare hearers to receive something that does nourish that charity. Such stories are likely to be harsher, with a hard edge, compared to stories that directly nourish charity. Listeners are far less likely to experience delight when hearing these stories. These stories, sadly, are more likely also to come from our news media.

Here is a (sadly factual) sample story I used in the early part of an address on the role of the family. I wanted very much to recognize that families as they exist in a sometimes broken and fallen world are not unambiguous blessings and to avoid a near idolatry of the family common in certain Christian circles. This story seems effectively to picture a negative reality about families at their worst.

The Kidnapping

A Missouri mother is behind bars today after police allege she plotted to have her six-year-old boy kidnapped in order to scare him because he is apparently "too nice" to people.

What happened on Monday must have been more than scary for the young boy, as the police department's accounting of events is disturbing.

The Lincoln County sheriff's office said the boy was lured into a man's truck on Monday after getting off his school bus.

The driver, Nathan Wynn Firoved, is a coworker of the boy's aunt, Denise Kroutil. The boy's mother, 25-year-old Elizabeth Hupp, Kroutil, and the grandmother, Rose Brewer, had earlier agreed to arrange the kidnapping to teach him a life lesson, police say.

Here's how events unfolded according to the sheriff's office:

Once in the truck, the young boy was told by Firoved that he would never see his mother again and he would be "nailed to the wall of a shed." When he started crying, Firoved showed him a gun and said he would be hurt if he didn't stop crying. He tied up the boy's hands and feet with plastic bags, and threw a jacket over his head so he could not see. The boy could not stop crying.

He was brought to his own house and put in the basement, where his aunt removed his pants and told him he would be sold into sex slavery. She was angry with the boy that he did not resist her actions, according to the police report.

After a few hours, the boy was allowed to go upstairs and his relatives lectured him about the danger posed by strangers.

"Family members told investigators their primary intent was to educate the victim and felt they did nothing wrong," the sheriff's department said in a statement.

The boy reported what happened to him to authorities at his school and they contacted the Division of Family Services. The boy is now in protective custody.[5]

Sometimes the real danger is not strangers. It is our own families.

Of course, the address did not end there. Stories such as this are most useful early in a sermon or lesson that has a movement from "bad news" to "good news." They picture for us the bad news that so marks a world with a seemingly absent or distant God. Sadly, it is often easier to illustrate the bad-news side of such an address so that our listeners fail to make the turn into the good news and simply slide off into the encompassing gloom. Such stories should normally, therefore, appear early in the sermon or lesson.

Trouble with a Sermon

I have always emphasized to my preaching students from early in my teaching career that they should look for the "trouble" in the text. That is to say,

5. Fitzpatrick, "Missouri Mom."

*they should identify what can surprise the preacher and likely the congrega-
tion and make them uncomfortable. It is here that there might be a point of
contact between the world of the text and the world of the listener. We might
even look for what is offensive in the text. As an example of this in my first
year as a teacher, I mentioned Luke 14, a chapter in which, it has always
seemed to me, Jesus behaves with genuine discourtesy to his hosts. I may not,
however, have made it clear that we normally go beyond this bad news to
some good news in the text.*

*Shortly after that lecture, one of the students in the class was preaching
in a church where a friend of mine was the minister. Apparently she had had
taken the lecture to heart for, I was told, the text of the sermon was drawn
from Luke 14. The sermon could be summarized as, "Jesus was rude. We
should be rude also."*

*The elders of the church were appalled by this performance and at the
conclusion of the service of worship rushed to their minister to voice their
outrage. "Who's teaching preaching at the College these days?" they asked.
My friend conveyed that to me with great delight. Since then I have emphasized that we normally do not end our sermons with "trouble."*

All this may help us to use more effectively the stories available to
us, but it doesn't give any assistance in knowing what to say when we tell
a nonfactual story, especially if we cannot footnote the story. The great
preacher and storyteller Fred Craddock is reported to have advised students if they can't find a good story, "Make one up; Jesus did!" I have no
ethical trouble with that approach, though I am convinced from hard
experience that it is much more difficult to make up a good story than
one might think. It's actually much easier to find a good story than to
create one, as I have already noted.

But imagine that we actually do have the capacity to create our own
true story. Is it ethically acceptable to let people think that the story is also
factual? The question is essentially the same as representing something
we have found on the internet as factual when we very well know it is not,
or when we at least ought to reasonably guess that it is not. (Many stories
on the internet fall into this category.)

How can we signal that a story is not factual without the equivalent
of a footnote? One suggestion, to drawn from the oral tradition about
Fred Craddock, is to put in details that help the listener know what kind
of story you are telling. To begin a story, "Once upon a time . . ." is to
signal to listeners that they should not expect a factual account. It is the

classic introduction to a fairy tale, and no one expects a fairy tale to be factual. As a consequence, no one listens to a fairy tale the way one listens to the morning news. The introduction "Once upon a time . . ." signals to readers that they should listen to the story with expectation like those coming with a fairy tale.

Putting in obviously absurd details is another such signal.

"Daddy, we want to adopt that cat!"

"Adopt that cat? You already have eight cats, four dogs and a hippopotamus. We don't have room for another cat!"

This does not mean that all the details of a factual story need to be strictly accurate. As I've noted elsewhere, one good way to enliven a story is to create dialogue to carry along the narrative. That need not be strictly accurate. So, for example, in "The Christmas Allan Was Fourteen," the story as a whole is factual and accurate, but I cannot claim that "Sheila" said exactly the words I put in her mouth. But those words do represent in a nonverbatim way the part she actually played in the story as a whole. I think this practice is ethically appropriate. The exception to this statement happens when a quotation becomes key to the point of the story. In that case the dialogue has to be as accurate as possible.

"The Christmas Allan Was Fourteen" and the companion story, "The Christmas Daniel Was in India," illustrate another point. We preachers very frequently use stories about our own children and other family members. We should check with them and gain their permission, as I have done with both Allan and Daniel, in order to avoid embarrassing them. If a story involves strangers, it can often be disguised sufficiently so that confidentiality is not violated. Disguising a story about our own family is not always possible. Telling a story should never cause our family pain or embarrassment.

And, of course, our stories must never, ever, violate pastoral confidentiality. That would constitute clergy malpractice.

BUT IS IT YOUR STORY?

As my father told me, you can't footnote a story. One important academic function of the footnote, however, is to name the source of information. Footnotes ensure an author's integrity. The parallel task in storytelling presents a problem, however. To claim a story as your own, even indirectly, is unethical. On the other hand, to give a lengthy, footnote-like description of its origin is tedious. Imagine that you decide to use one of the stories in this book in a sermon or lesson. "This story comes from a book written by a Canadian Presbyterian preacher and teacher named Stephen Farris," you say; and you give proper bibliographical information about the publication of the book. This level of detail would be more than boring in a sermon or lesson. Normally in storytelling, the source of a story is named for a specific reason. For example, the story may come from someone known either personally or by reputation to the listeners. Or the originator of the story may be so authoritative and respected that the story carries more weight if the originator is named. Or perhaps an event in the life or circumstances of the story's source makes the tale particularly compelling or ironic. In such circumstances, the storyteller's identity is part of the story. In other circumstances, something like "I heard a story," or "I read a story" is usually enough.

Such a practice would have prevented an instance of storytelling dishonesty that still grates on my memory.

Grandma Peterkin

Grandma Peterkin was an elderly lady in my boyhood congregation. Life had not been easy for her. Her husband had passed away, and her only son went down with a torpedoed merchant vessel in World War II. She lived with Mrs. Bennett, her only daughter. Grandma Peterkin adopted a grandmotherless boy in that church. She cared for him, asked after him, followed his development with interest, and, above all, prayed for him. When he decided to become a minister and went away to seminary, she wrote him the most beautiful and loving letters. (You know the name of the boy. I wish I had been wise enough to keep those letters.) One day when he was studying in England, a letter came from the familiar address but in different handwriting. The young man knew what the letter would say even before he opened it, and indeed he had guessed correctly. Mrs. Bennett was writing to say that Grandma had died. It happened this way: Mrs. Bennett was awakened in the night by a noise from Grandma's bedroom. She had knocked on the door, entered and asked,

"Mother, is everything all right?"

And Grandma replied, "Oh yes dear, I'm just dying."

She who believes has eternal life and has passed from death to life. The one who lives now in the age to come will continue to live in the age to come, even through death.

Here is the distressing part of the story: One year I told that story in class, and in the following year I heard or heard of three student sermons that included a story the preachers claimed was about their own grandmother, who when she was dying, said . . . I felt like jumping up and shouting, "Not true! I'm not worried about whether or not you credit me with the story, but it is profoundly dishonest to claim that the story is about your own grandmother. And it dishonors Grandma Peterkin, who was a very real and very loving Christian woman. Don't do that kind of thing!"

It is vital, then, to tell the truth when telling a story. One way of not telling the truth is not to tell the whole story; another way not to tell the truth is to keep on telling the same story in the same way when circumstances change. Here is a story that is both true and factual. I told it in a sermon I preached in the summer of 2007 on Hosea 11:1-9 . "When Israel was a child I loved him / . . . / How can I give you up?"

The Son

I have a friend who has told this story publicly himself and has given me permission to tell it also. He and his wife adopted a child, the son of a drug-addicted prostitute. They loved that child. They gave that child every opportunity and every gift. They poured out their love upon that boy. But things went wrong and he became addicted to drugs and to alcohol and financed that addiction by crime. He served time in federal penitentiary in the U.S. and in halfway houses in Canada. My friend told me about it, and his words were like Hosea's words. They dripped with love; they poured with pain. We love and things go wrong. There's pain and there's love and it's hard to know which is uppermost.

My friend told me that when his older son died, on the weekend of the funeral, his younger son, in a halfway house at the time, left the halfway house and burgled his family home during the funeral. I could hardly hear the story without my heart breaking, and I can hardly imagine how my friends' already broken hearts broke again when they returned home that day.

Well, my friend's son did his time in prison. His father and his mother visited and kept loving him. He broke the habit, all the habits. He found something that he was good at, a niche in life, and that niche was teaching English as a second language. He went to China to get a job there, a respectable job, teaching English in one of the great cities of China, and there he met a Chinese woman. He fell in love with her, and last February they got married and, of course, he invited his parents to come to the wedding. As father and son were walking through the streets of that great city, the son turned to the father and said "I'm sorry. I am sorry."

My friends never gave up. And neither, neither, does God.

I ended the sermon shortly thereafter. Later that year, however, I ran into that friend again and I asked him how his son was doing. The sad response was that he has gotten back into drugs, abandoned his wife, and, his father feared, might be selling drugs to support his habit. My friend was deeply worried that the son would be jailed in China, and who knows how Westerners fare in prison there? More recently still, I had another conversation with my friend. His son had indeed been arrested and is serving a sentence, just as my friend had feared.

It is dishonest only to tell stories that turn out well or to use them as sentimental veils over the messiness of life. It would be even more dishonest to keep on telling the story the same way I first did even though I now know that, at least for now, things have not turned out well for the young man.

Of course, my friend still loves his son. He and his wife are permitted one telephone call per week to the prison in China, and each week they make that call. And God still loves us, and even if my friend gives up (which would be understandable, though I do not think he will ever do so in this life), God will not give up. God still makes the call. That surely remains true. But I must not pretend that this is a success story of forgiveness any longer.

All this suggests a few guidelines for ethical storytelling:

1. Acquire a rule of faith or core interpretive principle that will help you determine what is true.

2. Do not pretend a story is factual if it is not.

3. Be honest but brief about where you found your story.

4. Maintain pastoral confidentiality.

5. Check with family members in particular before telling stories about them.

6. Don't keep telling a story if the circumstances around the story have changed radically.

The theological trouble with rules, even ones we more gently name guidelines, is that only a person of good character can follow them. These all come down to something like, be honest about your storytelling. An honest person can follow that rule, but a dishonest person?

An interesting theme recurs from time to time in ancient writings about rhetoric: the character of speakers matters as much as their skills. The skills of rhetoric, and of storytelling, can only be rightly practiced by a person of good character. From this insight comes one of the best-known classical descriptions of rhetoric, "A good [person] speaking well."[6] What the ancients called virtue matters in storytelling as in everything else.

Of course, as a Christian, I believe that a good character of a Christian person comes from the work of the Spirit of Christ in us. If you do have to choose between being an effective storyteller and a good Christian, choose to be a good Christian. It may be, in the mercy of God, that being a good Christian might even make you a better storyteller. This work does curve back upon itself. The Holy Spirit imprints the work of Christ upon us through the stories of Jesus and the many other stories that cluster around them. Ethical storytelling involves taking these stories to heart.

Blisters on the Larynx and Other Problems of the Voice

Many years ago, when I was a very new and still wet-behind-the-lecture-notes professor of homiletics, I was invited to participate in a conference on the techniques of voice production. The conference was jointly organized by the Pathology Department of the Faculty of Medicine of the University of Toronto and by the Voice Department of the Royal Conservatory of Music of Toronto. In short, it was being run on the one hand by professionals who educate those who depend completely on good voice production for a living and, on the other hand, by those who try to heal us if we damage our voices in some way. In fact, at the time, they told us that they could diagnose serious problems very accurately but there was very little they could actually do to cure the more serious problems. With respect to those health problems, prevention rather than cure was the watchword of the program. It still is.

The program was fascinating. It featured, for example, full-color photos of the blood blisters on the larynx of a lounge singer who had seriously

---

6. Quintilian, *Institutio Oratoria*, 12.1.1. In this definition Quintilian is apparently following an earlier Roman orator, Cato the Elder. It is also true in storytelling that we often draw from those who have gone before us.

overstrained his voice. There was an amazing video produced while inserting both a camera and a strobe light down the throat of a singer in full flight. The strobe light slowed down the appearance of the waves in the skin of the larynx to the point at which they were visible in the camera. The waves are incredibly fine but they shape the quality of the human voice. Blisters such as the lounge singer's interrupt the waves and damage the voice. Moreover, the scar tissue that remains after the blisters have supposedly healed can remain in place and inhibit those waves. Very little can be done about that scar tissue. I have no idea how anyone can sing with a camera and strobe light down the throat. But one thing, I knew: the presenters at this conference were experts in their fields.

That made my job more daunting. I had been invited as a teacher of preaching to participate in a panel composed of representatives of professions which depend on the use of the voice. (Sadly, another reason for my presence is that the organizers had found that preachers are among those who most commonly abuse and damage their voices through faulty voice production.) At the end of the panel presentation, the moderator asked each of us to offer one key piece of advice to the audience. What could I say to the conference that had not already been said more authoritatively and more compellingly by others?

Just one thing: "Only use your voice to speak the truth."

5

Through the Year in the Church

There is both an official church year, laid out in service books and scholarly works on the liturgy, and what might be called a real church year. The official church year, beginning with Advent, moves through Christmas, Epiphany and so on, all the way to Christ the King Sunday, and should be observed. There is also a real church year, which will vary from place to place but is, well, real. Some of the major feasts of the real church year do not appear in the official church year. Neither Mother's Day, Remembrance Day in Canada or Memorial Day in the U.S. nor Rally Day (when Sunday school starts up again the autumn) appears in the official church year but these celebrations are in their respective nations, vital parts of the real church year.

Some events in the official year, however, do make it into the real church year. Christmas, for example, belongs both to the official church year and to the real church year. But Christmas occurs after December 25 in the official year and before it in the real church year, at least in many places. If you doubt that assertion, listen to the radio stations to hear when they play Christmas music. Or simply keep track of church attendance. This is not a matter to be held in scorn. It is very possible that the church authorities placed Christmas just after the solstice in the first place, not because they thought Jesus had been born at that time of year, but because there was a celebration out there in pagan society and its calendar. In other words they accommodated to the actual calendar by which Christians lived within the wider society, something very like a real church year. They wanted to give Christians something to do other than eating, drinking and partying. I have to say that the pagans may be winning this one.

In the real church year, the life of the church intersects with the life of the wider society. Woe to the priest, minister, or pastor who ignores the real church year. In many congregations of my own tradition, a minister could inadvertently forget Pentecost and few would notice. But if that minister forgets Mother's Day, trouble is coming!

Taking note of the real church year is not simply a matter of clerical self-preservation. Church life moves from the outside in: we invite people from wider society into the life of the church, a life shaped, at its best, by the mighty acts of God and by events in the life of Jesus, which structure the church year. The rhythms of that life are repeated when we observe the official church year. Church life also moves from the inside out as the gospel moves into the life of the whole society. This second direction is harder to manage, but it is just as important. This direction—from the inside out—is the direction of the incarnation. Give thanks that we don't have to choose between the two directions. We ought to be able to hold them in creative tension.

ADVENT

First Advent

I received an invitation some years ago to preach on the first Sunday of Advent in a church which did carefully observe the official church year. It was at that time a church which maintained the older practice in many Protestant churches of placing the sermon as the last major item in the order of service. The worship bulletin had been prepared before I submitted a sermon title so at that point in the service it read:

Sermon Rev. Dr. Stephen Farris

Hymn

Organ Postlude: Sleepers Awake!

A friend bustled up to me after the service, pointed to the bulletin and told me, delight on his face, "They certainly knew you were coming!"

One detail in this story illustrates an ethical problem in storytelling. For the purposes of this book, I have written the story exactly as it happened.

It is as factual as I could make it. But I often tell the story slightly differently. Most churches in my tradition, including the congregation where this incident took place, have now moved the sermon to a time nearer the midpoint of the order of service. This happened so many years ago that many people either do not know or have forgotten that we once did things differently. Explaining the situation orally takes time and impedes the flow of the story with unnecessary detail. Nowadays, I usually just say that the worship bulletin read this way:

Sermon Rev. Dr. Stephen Farris

Hymn: Sleepers Awake!

I smooth out the story by altering a minor detail. How much of that smoothing out process can be done with integrity when we tell our stories? I think that this particular change is acceptable. On the other hand, it would not do to fit "Sleepers Awake" into the story if that hymn had not been played in the real-life situation. But responsible storytellers will have to decide these matters for themselves.

The Christmas Pageant

If you still doubt the assertion that Christmas occurs before December 25 in the real church year, ask yourself why so many churches hold their Christmas pageants some time before December 25. Of course, if you are a purist on behalf of the official year, you could hold the Christmas pageant at some point in the official twelve days of Christmas. And good luck to you with that project.

In my first church, we did hold a Christmas pageant, at the usual time of year. It featured the usual shepherds in their fathers' bathrobes, striped tea towels tied to their heads, a thrilled young girl as the Virgin Mary, a less thrilled boy looking on as Joseph, bearded with cotton batten, leaning on a staff to keep from falling over, and a large doll, wrapped in swaddling clothes and laid in a manger. The youngest children in the church were the sheep, all of them wearing either black or white balaclavas to which sheep ears had been sewn. In defiance of proper liturgical practice, the magi had also made an early appearance, instead of waiting for Epiphany. They wore colorful robes and cardboard crowns covered with leftover gold wrapping paper. At the dress rehearsal, however, the three magi steadfastly refused to stand where the director of the pageant had instructed them to take their places. The director, patience tried very near the breaking point, made her way forward to deal with this insubordination when suddenly one of the sheep let out a loud wail and ran for the exit. Then the director noticed that there was a large and spreading yellow tinged puddle, just where the magi had been supposed to stand. It turns out that a little lamb had done what sheep do in real life and that the magi were wise men indeed.

But perhaps that particular pageant was closer than usual to the essence of Christmas. I am speaking of Christmas not as it appears on greeting cards or even in more orderly pageants. I am speaking of the feast of the incarnation, an incarnation which, according to the much-loved story in Luke, began in a stable. And stables do smell of, well, several things.

A Christmas Eve Communion

There was a particularly lovely lady in my first church, Meg, who was dying slowly of cancer through the fall and winter of the year. Her daughter had wandered the world and had done things that wounded her mother and father, Robert, deeply. Between them there had grown up a coldness, but that winter, bitter both for its cold and for the chill of impending death, the daughter came home, to see her dying mother. Between the Christmas services in the church, I took my little leather portable communion kit on a pastoral visit to Meg and her daughter. Like so much in my life, the kit was an inheritance from my father, and given to me by my mother. It was, in its own way, a symbol to me of a loving relationship between parent and child. I did not mention that, of course.

After some conversation, I judged that it would be appropriate to celebrate communion, brought out the kit and prepared the Lord's Table in the sickroom.

"This is my body given for you," I said, and the three of us shared the bread.

"This is the new covenant in my blood, shed for the forgiveness of sins."

And mother and daughter began to weep and embraced each other. There was no cure that night, but let no one deny that there was a healing.

I have no trouble remembering the date of Meg's eventual death, for it occurred the night after the birth of our second son, Daniel. Daniel was born after a long and difficult labor, late on a Saturday evening, and Robert called me to say that Meg had finally passed away very late the next day, on Sunday. I went over to the home and watched while their excellent family doctor pronounced Meg dead. The husband, the doctor, and the minister sat down in the living room. The husband put on his favorite music, pan pipes as I recall, and served a drink for us all. We drank to Meg's memory and sat for several hours, doing very little but chatting from time to time.

The next day I visited Patty and our new son in the hospital. Patty showed me a lovely bouquet, obviously ordered the day before. The card said, "From Meg and Robert."

Life and death are sometimes very close together.

CHRISTMAS STORIES

There is no better time to tell stories, or to hear them, than at Christmas. So here are a few stories for the season . . .

The Christmas Allan Was Fourteen

I remember the year my son Allan was fourteen . . . and a typical, grumpy fourteen-year-old he was. At that time the youth group in our Toronto-area church was led by a theology student named Doug, and Allan would attend, sometimes under protest, but attending under protest is probably as good as it gets with fourteen-year-old boys. Just before Christmas Doug announced that there would be a special Christmas Bible Study and party. Because the Weight Watchers group was meeting in the church that evening, he announced that the study would be held in the house of Shel, one of the elders of the church.

"Meet in the parking lot of the church and we'll drive to Shel's house," announced Doug.

That evening was cold and precisely that miserable temperature at which the rain can't decide whether it's actually snow or not. After waiting for the usual stragglers, the group set off for Shel's house. They gathered in the driveway and waited in the sleet as Doug knocked on the door. Shel came to the door and said "Yes? Can I help you?"

"We're scheduled to hold our Bible study here because the church is full. Surely you remember!"

"I'm sorry," said Shel. "There must be some mistake. My son is back from university and is having a party with his friends. It's just not possible."

Doug stumped back down the drive and told the group the news. They grumbled a bit and he said, "Why don't we try the manse. They'll let us in there!"

They all piled into the car and drove the few blocks to the manse. Once again the group waited in the driveway as Doug knocked on the door. This time they were just a little wetter and a little more impatient. Dana, the minister's wife, came to the door and Doug explained the situation.

"So, can we meet here?"

"I'm sorry." Dana replied. "Our son has an earache and our daughter isn't very well either. I'm afraid it just isn't possible."

Now the grumbling was even louder, and Doug looked very puzzled indeed as he returned back down the drive.

"I guess we could try my parents' house" said Doug. "It's not very far away and they might let us in." So the kids piled pack into the cars and drove to the parents' house. Once again, the teens waited in the driveway as Doug knocked on the door. His mother, Sheila, came to the door and Doug almost begged to be let in.

"Mom, Weight Watchers is in the church tonight so we were supposed to hold our special Christmas Bible Study at Shel's house, but his son was having a party with his friends. So we couldn't hold the meeting there. And Dana's children are sick, so we couldn't hold the meeting at the manse. Could we please use this house?"

"Now Douglas, you'll just have to learn to plan better than that. I'm sorry. It's just not possible. We had new windows put in the house today and it's covered with sawdust. You can't come in here."

Doug begged his mother to change her mind and finally she relented— relented a very little.

"I'll tell you what. The garage is empty right now and it's clean and dry. You can use the garage if you want."

"The garage! Who does she think we are!" thought the teens. But they were cold and wet and certainly, nothing better was on offer.

So Doug walked over to the big double garage door, grasped its handle and slid the door back.

Inside the garage was a Christmas tree, chairs and on a small table, a crèche, a model of the stable in Bethlehem."

"It got to me," said Allan when he came home and told us about the evening. "For the first time, it got to me."

May Christmas, and all the love it represents, "get to you" this year.

The Christmas Daniel was in India

At Christmastime in 2007 my son Daniel, having graduated from univer-sity, was travelling through India, by himself, with no tasks to do; he was definitely not a pilgrim; he was not seeking enlightenment from the ancient wisdom of the east; he was simply a traveler. He was journeying through cen-tral India, by train where possible and by bus where it was not, well off the beaten tourist track. A third-class train ticket is easily within the means even of a Western traveler spending his money very carefully, and a bus is even cheaper. Daniel intended to pass Christmas Day in a small town in about the place your forefinger would land if you tried to point to the geographical center of India on a map. Though Daniel's destination was hardly a tourist magnet to match the Taj Mahal, it was large enough to warrant an entry in the Lonely Planet guidebook, and he had managed to secure his accommoda-tion for Christmas Eve in an inn listed in his guide. The Lonely Planet, it appears, reaches even into off the beaten track towns in India.

Either the town itself or possibly the place where Daniel had passed the night of December 23 was so far off that beaten track, however, that travel by bus was necessary. The bus ride to his destination was supposed to be a seven-hour journey. Daniel arrived at the bus station just before the sched-uled time of departure, climbed aboard the bus and waited and waited. The bus simply sat there, becoming more and more jammed by the minute. By the time the bus got underway, many hours late, he was wedged onto the end of a bench that had been designed for two people but was now accommodating, to use the word very loosely, three other men in addition to Daniel and one very sick boy. The boy, it became apparent, was the young son of the man sitting next to Daniel. The child had obviously thrown up, probably several times judging by the smell, at least once in the very recent past. The boy was lying across the four men on the bench, including Daniel.

As the bus journeyed on through the gathering dark, Daniel stared down at the boy. He took note of the gaunt face and the foam escaping from the corner of the boy's lips. He began to form the opinion that the boy might be dying, but, to Daniel's surprise, the boy's father didn't seem particularly anxious. Daniel tried to communicate his fears to the father. "How long has he been sick? Don't you think he should see a doctor?" Daniel wanted to ask. But the father knew no English, and Daniel's Hindi was confined to a few phrases gleaned from a guidebook. Guidebooks can teach you how to book a room in a hotel or buy a ticket to Delhi, but they can never offer instruction in human concern. So Daniel sat there as, with painful slowness, falling farther behind schedule by the minute, the bus jolted its way through the heart of India. At one unnamed, unknown village the father gathered up his sick son, climbed down into the enveloping darkness and was gone. And the bus rolled on.

Many hours later the bus arrived at Daniel's destination. He made his way to his inn, knocked on the door and the innkeeper appeared.

"It's so very late. We did not think you would arrive, so we gave away your room. My apologies, but all the rooms are now full," explained the innkeeper apologetically.

"I will phone around the other hotels and inns but there is a festival and many people are travelling. I am not hopeful."

His prediction was correct. There appeared to be not a single vacancy in the town. But Daniel had learned that sometimes a no on the telephone can become a face-to-face yes, so he decided to try for himself. It didn't work this time. He wandered the streets of this godforsaken little town, all alone, and every hotel and inn held only a No for him. As he walked the streets he thought of his Christmases past and the story he had been taught as a child. But in that Hindu town he suspected that he was likely the only person who could recognize the irony. Alone in a far country at Christmas, and there was no room in the inn.

What happened to my son? "Come back here if you can find nothing," the innkeeper had told him. After hours of useless searching, Daniel decided to return to the inn where he had made his reservation. The innkeeper had realized that a number of his guests were in the same party and had persuaded two of them to share a room. For Daniel, though not for Jesus, there was indeed room in the inn.

What happened to that other man's son, the one on the bus? Who knows? And who cares? My son was fine.

Who cares? God does—and that's the Christmas message.

It turns out that this is not such a lonely planet after all. For ever since Bethlehem, there is no such thing as a God-forsaken little place.

The Wine Glass

My wife, Patty, and I returned from graduate study in England in the autumn of 1981 debt free but nearly penniless and with a six-month-old baby to support. That is not at all a complaint, let me tell you. Penniless but debt free is better off than most graduate students. Moreover, at least I knew that a job was awaiting me. I had been appointed under the old Ordained Missionary system, to Trinity Church, Amherstview, Ontario. What's more, Trinity Church had a manse. A job, or better, a ministry, an assured income, a home to live in—who could ask for anything more? Well, it turns out that a family setting up a home for the first time does demand a few things more. The income was assured, but it was also low. As a newly ordained minister, I was on "minimum stipend with no annual increments," which in plain English meant "not all that much."

We collected furniture from the attics of all our relatives, I believe "Early Attic" is both the name of a kind of ancient Greek pottery and of a furniture style widely displayed in the homes of new clergy and other impecunious folk. We scraped together a down payment for a car and applied for a credit card. The bank authorities turned us down; our income was too low. The local bank manager personally interceded for us, however, and in due course, we did receive a shiny but very limited credit card. We had been granted what I believe was the lowest possible credit limit at that time: two hundred dollars.

But life was good. I was enjoying the ministry. The church took a few modest steps forward, and after living in dorm rooms, student flats, and apartments for our entire married life, it felt good to have to lock both a front and a back door at night. A year soon passed by, and the Christmas of 1982 approached—the end of my first full year of ministry. Buying presents on minimum stipend and with a two-hundred-dollar credit limit was a challenge. But we managed, barely. It was all made a little easier by the fact that we didn't need to cook a Christmas dinner. Trinity Church held two Christmas Eve services but none on the day itself. Our plan was to drive first thing in the morning to Patty's parents' home to spend Christmas with the extended family. So the cupboard and fridge were all but bare: no cake, no fruit, no goodies, no Christmas cheer.

My only real difficulty was that I had not yet bought Patty a present, and Christmas Day was approaching. The morning of Christmas Eve itself had come before I could find the time to go shopping for her. I drove through the ice and snow of the Ontario winter to the nearest mall and began to scout around. The limit on our credit card had long been reached and I had a little less than twenty-five dollars in cash in my pocket. Any present for Patty had to be less than that hard-and-fast limit. The amazing thing is that I actually found a gift for her, a box of six not particularly lovely but satisfactorily inexpensive wineglasses. It was perhaps not the wisest gift since there would certainly not be enough left actually to purchase a bottle of wine to go with them. But at least Patty could open the box, admire them and place them in the sparsely covered shelves in our kitchen. So I paid for the wineglasses—with cash, of course—and made my way through the icy parking lot to the car.

I shifted my weight to transfer the box of glasses to my left hand, reached for my keys, slipped on the ice, and fell flat on my face beside the driver's side door. I could hear what I had done to the wineglasses but I didn't even have the heart to look. I drove home with self-pity buckled up beside me in the passenger seat. I had worked so hard. I had studied so long. I didn't have a single goody in the house to celebrate with my wife and new son, not even a bottle of wine, and now I had smashed my wife's Christmas present.

I opened the door and stepped into the manse's front hall. Patty had been watching for me and grasped immediately that there was something wrong; she could hear me clinking. There didn't seem to be any point in hiding the disaster from her. I said, "Patty love, I bought you some wineglasses for Christmas but I slipped on the ice in the parking lot. You can hear what happened." And I held out the box to her.

Patty rubbed me gently and soothingly on the arm and said, "It doesn't matter, my love. Let's open up and see if any survived." And there, amidst the shards, there remained two intact wineglasses! One for Patty, one for me, who could ask for anything more?

Just then we could hear the mailbox lift and clang shut. I stepped outside and retrieved the mail: flyers, some belated Christmas cards and, to my surprise, an envelope from the headquarters of the Presbyterian Church in Canada. Inside there was a letter stating that a donor who wished to remain anonymous had established a fund to give a helping hand, especially at Christmas, to ministers paid at or near minimum stipend. Inside the letter was a check for $387.00.

Christmas Eve, a gift I had not expected and could not deserve, Christmas Eve!

There was just enough time to rush to the bank, deposit the check, withdraw a little cash, pick up some fruit and shortcake and, above all, get to the wine store to buy one bottle of inexpensive wine.

That night after the second service was over and Allan was soundly asleep, Patty set out the fruit and shortcake. I opened the wine bottle and carefully filled our two new wineglasses. A connoisseur would turn up his educated nose at the wine, and the glasses were less than fine crystal, but in the candlelight the wine glowed like richest rubies. We sat together on the long-used, hand-me-down couch, sampled the fruit and sipped our wine, Then, with a contented sigh, Patty put down her glass, stretched out her legs to snuggle into my shoulder....

And kicked over her wineglass.

We have moved many times since that Christmas Eve and over the years we have been given or purchased some very fine glassware indeed. But in our china cabinet there sits to this very day one rather plain, perhaps even ugly, but treasured wineglass.

That source of help for clergy is called the Fund for Ministerial Assistance. I hear they are a little short of money this year. And that may be the case with whatever is the equivalent fund in your church.

The story found in the conclusion of chapter 1, "The Socks," is a winter story rather than a Christmas story, but it also seems to fit well at Christmas.

ORDINARY TIME

A Winter Sunday: The Good Samaritan

On a winter Sunday I was scheduled to preach at a church north of Toronto. It was a cold, icy morning and, as happens too often, I did not quite leave enough time for a comfortable journey to my destination. Murphy's traffic law applied that day—the one that states that the more you are in a hurry, the greater the probability that any given traffic light will turn red as you approach it. That was certainly the case at a large intersection on my way: six lanes by four lanes and very much exposed to the weather. An older gentleman crossed the intersection in front of me, limping noticeably on his cane. The light turned orange for him as he neared the opposite sidewalk, and then red, so he quickened his pace. In his hurry he planted his cane on a patch of ice and fell heavily to the ground.

Everything else I am now about to tell you about the incident happened in the moment of time that it took me to put the transmission into park and reach for the door handle. I thought, "Oh no, he may be hurt. I'll have to stop and see if he is all right. I may even have to take him to the emergency room." We all know, of course, how long you might have to wait in an emergency room these days. "I'll be terribly late for church. I might not even make it."

I could picture the ushers checking their watches, the organist playing the prelude . . . for the third time, the elders with their heads together, whispering to one another, "He has cut it close sometimes but he has never been this late!" Finally, in desperation, they draw straws to determine who would be stuck conducting the service in my absence.

In the midst of these unexpressed grumbles, however, a phrase from a story came to my mind. I was first told the story as a small child and over the years it's been repeated to me many times. It's a well-known story (you've heard it too), and you have all heard a phrase from it: "And he passed by on the other side."

I don't actually have to say anything more to you than that phrase. Because it is a life-shaping story, all I have to say to you is, "And he passed by on the other side." That is the way it is with life-shaping stories; an allusion is enough. The whole story comes to your mind and you understand the connection to my little tale. Partly because I have heard that story so many times, from Bible stories read by my mother, from Sunday school lessons, from sermons I have heard and from sermons I have preached, I am the person I am. I could not "pass by on the other side" and be the person I am.

Far more important, I knew with confidence that this story would also come to the minds of the people in the congregation whose service I was planning to lead that morning. As the kind of story that comes automatically to mind, it also had shaped who they were. If I phoned from the emergency room and explained my situation, they would understand my absence. The organist would begin a congregational hymnsing. The elders would choose someone to pray, someone to read the lessons and perhaps even to reflect on them. No one would say, "He ought to have passed by on the other side." Who were these people? They were the kind of people who knew the story of the Good Samaritan and had let it shape their actions and attitudes. They could not expect their Sunday preacher to pass by on the other side and still be the people they were. There is a word for people who have been shaped by this story and others like it. That word is church.

By the way, before I had fully opened the door, the old gentleman had staggered to his feet. He glared at me as if daring me to take notice of his tumble, and stumped away. I drove on and even made it to church on time.

As I drove on to church that day, I thought about what had happened in me. I had realized that I had been shaped by a story I knew so well that even a phrase brought the whole to mind. Then I thought about the children in the church to which I was driving through the blowing snow. What stories did they know so well that even a phrase would bring them to mind? Probably not stories from the Bible! More likely they would only know that thoroughly scenes from movies or from TV. This little winter's tale of mine took place while *Seinfeld* was the top-rated TV show. I wondered if the children would know the story behind "Yadda, yadda, yadda" better than, "he passed by on the other side." And what would a society shaped by "Yadda, yadda, yadda" look like? Oddly enough, the writers of *Seinfeld* actually reflected on just that question in the final episode of the series. I am not against knowing TV shows, especially well-written ones! I am for knowing the Good Samaritan and other Bible stories.

As a result of all this, I resolved to retell the story of the Good Samaritan that day in the church. Since preachers are not expected to send in titles of children's stories in time for the printing of the worship bulletin, I was free to tell the parable of the Good Samaritan during children's time. I told the Bible story as vigorously and winningly as I could. Some months later, as spring spread through the countryside, the congregation called a new minister, and one of the elders thanked me warmly for preaching during the vacancy.

"We'll always remember your preaching," she said. "I am sure none of us will ever forget your sermon on the Good Samaritan!"

Except it wasn't a sermon. It was just a story. But sometimes a story is enough.

Bob's Story

This story was told to me by Bob's mother.

As a student of theology, I passed an intern year or "Student in Ministry" year in a small town in West Virginia. West Virginia is to this day one of the poorest American states, but in the late 1930s it was very poor indeed. Nobody in that town was wealthy, and that definitely included Bob's family. Now, young Bob wanted very much to be a medical doctor. He hung on the heels of Dr. Laird, the town's much-loved physician. When he was old enough, he would accompany Dr. Laird on his rounds, prepare his equipment, and clean and sterilize it after the various procedures carried out in those days by a hardworking medical practitioner. Bob was made to be a doctor, but unfortunately there was simply no way on God's green earth that his family could afford to send him to the university for the long years of a medical education. When Bob graduated from high school, Dr. Laird called him into his office and told him,

"Bob, I believe that you have what it takes to be an excellent doctor. I know your family cannot afford a medical education, so I intend to pay what it costs for you to go through med school."

And Dr. Laird did just that. He paid the bill for his protégé.

When Bob finally graduated, he returned to his hometown before taking up his internship. Of course, he went to see his old mentor and benefactor.

"I will have a small income for the next two years but I would like to make arrangements to pay you back for all your kindness to me."

But Dr. Laird refused. "There is no way that you can ever pay me back for what I have done for you. But this is what you can do: one day you will meet a young person who was made to be doctor but can't afford the education. And you will pay what it costs to turn that young person into a doctor."

We can never pay back what God has given us. But perhaps we can pay on . . . to others. Perhaps that is what it means to love our neighbors as ourselves.

The Good Shepherd: "Through"

As a young man I worked several summers under the supervision of a minister named Alex a half generation older than I was. Alex and I shared a common origin; both of us were sons of Presbyterian ministers. The two fathers had also known each other, and in fact my father had served on the board of the inner-city mission that Alex's father had founded. One day Alex mentioned to me that my father had participated in his father's funeral.

"I'll never forget something your father said at the funeral. He read the 23rd Psalm."

Now, that scarcely counts as unusual or memorable. Psalm 23 is surely on the short list of Scripture passages most commonly read at funerals. But Alex explained what he meant.

"Of course, I knew the psalm well, but when your father read the psalm I heard something in it for the first time. He emphasized the word *through*—'through the valley of the shadow of death.' And even in my grief, I realized that it was not God's will that we should wander around in the valley of the shadow. God wants to lead us through the valley and out the other side. Through!"

My father was still alive then, so I asked him about the funeral and told him what Alex had said. "I don't recall doing that," said Dad. "I certainly did not do it on purpose, but Alex is right about the idea. *Through* is one of the most important words in the Bible." (This is another instance of meaning being created not just by the speaker but by the listener.)

A niggling little problem remained, however. I recalled that the much-loved hymn or metrical version of the psalm goes in the opposite direction in that verse "Yea, though I walk in death's dark vale . . . " So the question arose: What does the psalm actually say?

I got out my Hebrew Bible and an enormous Brown-Driver-Briggs Lexicon from my student days. (No, I did not have to blow off the dust!) The Hebrew was very simple; the preposition in question was the Hebrew letter *beth*. Biblical Hebrew is not rich in prepositions, and that preposition can be rendered many ways in English. But the most common translation is "in." This was not what I wanted. But I persevered, rooting through the various possibilities listed in the lexicon. Very near the end of the list of possible translations was a short note, stating that with verbs of motion, the preposition can often mean "into" or "through." Ah. Through. It is God's intention to bring us through our times of trouble and to the table rich with good things, the table of God's presence.

A Few Minutes as a Shepherd

It happens that I once had the opportunity to act as a shepherd for half an hour. At that point our family included Rupert, a young Australian Shepherd, barely more than a puppy at the time. Aussies, as they are called, look like large, tailless border collies with strikingly colored coats and are, despite their name, the ranch dog of the American southwest. They are bright, agile, energetic, and ready to learn. The breeder from whom we had bought Rupert let us know that there would be an "Aussie Fun Day" on a farm northeast of Toronto at which both dogs and their humans could try a range of activities. Among the possibilities was a half-hour experience of herding sheep. That sounded fascinating, and I put down our names for a session of herding sheep.

When we arrived at the farm and started walking towards the large paddock where the shepherding lessons were to be found, Rupert became visibly excited, shaking and straining at his leash. Obviously he had caught the scent of the sheep. He had never scented sheep in his life, nor in all probability had his sire and dam, but his instincts were telling him that something wonderful and exciting was just down the road.

Not all the Aussies had the herding instinct to the same level. As we arrived at the paddock, Rupert's full brother's turn with the sheep had come. There were three sheep, two ewes and a ram. Sheep are not the cute little lambykins of Sunday school lessons. They are smelly, solidly built and, at least to me, surprisingly large. The ram was bigger than the dog. He took one look at Rupert's brother and knocked him down, demonstrating very neatly the meaning of the verb "to ram." The dog got back to his feet and the ram knocked him down again. The shepherd called an end to the session. The dog clearly didn't have it, whatever "it" is in shepherding terms.

Now it was Rupert's turn. We entered the paddock as directed by the shepherd. Rupert trotted over to the sheep and caught the ram's eye. The ram turned away and huddled with the ewes. Rupert was clearly already in command. He had what shepherds call the "eye." My school principal wife says that some teachers have the school equivalent of the "eye" also. You either have it or you don't. Rupert had it.

Rupert had it, but I didn't. I needed instruction. The shepherd handed me her staff. It was surprisingly heavy with its bottom end shod in brass. From the pictures in the Sunday school materials of my childhood, I had always supposed that the business end of the staff was the crook. In my mind, I could picture the Good Shepherd reaching out to rescue a little white lambykin with the crook. Not so. The business end is the bottom end, with its heavy brass shoe. If protecting the sheep became necessary, the staff could make quite a weapon.

That did not prove necessary. But the shepherd did instruct me in its use. "Point with the staff to where you want the sheep to go. Walk up and down the field. The dog's job is to run in a U-shape around the sheep and keep them walking with you. If he starts misbehaving, give him a light whack with the staff. If he really misbehaves, you may have to stick it between his legs and trip him up."

I did as instructed and began to walk down the field. Rupert needed no instruction but kept the sheep close to me, running instinctually in the U-shape described by the shepherd. After a period of this exercise, the shepherd called a halt to the exercise and turned to me.

"This dog is a natural," she said. *"You have to put him in training for sheep dog trials."*

That would not be convenient for the pet of a family that lives in the middle of a large metropolitan area and, more important, in the middle of a sometimes hectic life. Putting the family pet into serious training was not on. I tried to explain this to the shepherd as politely as I could, but she persisted. Meanwhile, the sheep had wandered off far from the shepherd, as sheep are said to do, finding themselves behind a series of oil drums set up on end as an obstacle course. Still conversing with the eager shepherd, I raised the staff and pointed at the sheep. Rupert trotted off, gathered the sheep effortlessly from behind the oil drums and brought all three back to the shepherd and to me.

"See?" said the shepherd.

Well, I did see, but it didn't mean that we would put Rupert in training. He lived and eventually died as a much-loved family pet and never learned to be a champion sheep dog. I think I learned something from the experience however. Though there is no evidence that shepherds in biblical times used dogs in their work, they did have a staff.

"Thy rod and thy staff, they comfort me . . ." That is so. But perhaps it is sometimes a tough comfort, a tough love. The Good Shepherd protects us with the staff, points with it, and perhaps even gives us a whack with it when necessary. And, from my own experience, I am sure the Shepherd sticks the staff between our legs and trips us up when we head in the wrong direction.

Anything to get us through.

GOOD FRIDAY

Are You Saved?

From time to time I am asked by some earnest soul, "Are you saved?" My answer is, "I have been saved. I am being saved, and I will be saved." It would be a useful and not particularly difficult exercise for an adult or teen Bible study group to investigate the past, present, and future aspects of salvation.

Quite often, however, the above answer seems a little long and pretentious, so I simply respond, "Yes!" Perhaps it says something unfortunate about my character or reputation that my questioner generally seems astounded by my reply. Or perhaps it says something about the kind of person who asks the question. They never seem to believe me. "But when?" my interrogator will ask in an incredulous tone of voice. What this question really means is actually quite clear. The questioner wants to ask, "When did you commit your life to the Lord Jesus as your personal Savior?" He or she wants to know the particular point, at an evangelistic crusade or a summer camp, for example, at which I made a decision for Christ. And, since I have obviously not done so, he or she is willing to point me in the right direction at the very moment. In fact, I could give a perfectly respectable answer to this question also: "When I was sixteen, at the Scott Mission Camp, sitting on the diving board of the camp pool with the camp director." That's what an inherited family faith became real to me. I am not convinced, however, that this answer, though certainly vital for me biographically, is actually the most important one.

It is said that the great Swiss theologian Karl Barth was once asked this question also. His reported response was something like, "On a Friday afternoon, in the spring, outside the city of Jerusalem, in or about the year 30 AD."

That's a better answer. A good Calvinist might even echo the letter to the Ephesians and say, "Before the foundation of the world," in the will and purpose of God (cf. Eph 1:4). These answers suppose, rightly, that salvation is not primarily our work or the consequence of our own choices, important though those choices doubtless are. Our choice of God is made only in response to God's choice of us.

The good news is not really that I committed my life to the Lord Jesus Christ, significant though that is in my autobiography. It is that the Lord Jesus committed his life to me, and to the world.

By the way, this too is a story from oral tradition. I have not seen it in print in a scholarly book about Barth.

Jesus Loves Me

There is an even more famous tale about Barth, one that I have often seen in print and heard in sermons. It has been told so often that I only repeat it here because of the circumstances of the most memorable of the many times I heard the story. The story was once recounted in my hearing by a woman who claimed credibly and with the corroboration of others that the punch line had been said in response to her question. The lady in question was the wife of one of my professors at Union Theological Seminary in Richmond,

Virginia (now Union Presbyterian Seminary). The husband was not the terminally grumpy professor who will appear in several stories in this chapter, I hasten to add.

Karl Barth, it is thought, accepted the invitation to speak at the seminary largely because he was fascinated by the American Civil War and wanted to see the battlefields of that great struggle. Whether or not that is the case, he did deliver a very learned lecture at the seminary. It was so learned, in fact, that the lady in question understood scarcely a word of the lecture. She stood up in the question period and asked, "Dr. Barth, could you summarize your theology in one sentence?"

The audience gasped in horror than anyone could dare to ask the author of so many profound works to sum everything up in one sentence. But Barth surprised them.

"Certainly, Madam: 'Jesus loves me, this I know. For the Bible tells me so.'"

I have heard claims that Barth used that line on several other occasions. That may well be true. Experienced speakers are very likely to use a good line, or a good story, more than once.

Easter

A Soviet Easter

A friend of mine once traveled to the old Soviet Union shortly before the fall of communism. It happened that he was in St. Petersburg, then Leningrad, on Russian Orthodox Easter Sunday. He was told that there was a church near where he was staying, so he decided to walk to it for worship. To his surprise, in the officially atheist Soviet Union, many thousands of people were waiting outside the church. Though the church building was very large, with a capacity of several thousand worshipers, far more were waiting on the street than could be accommodated. Order was being kept by police guards.

At the appointed time, the priest and other celebrants began worship in the time-honored Orthodox manner, by leading a procession around the block. The procession was subdued, even mournful, representing the women on the way to the tomb to anoint the dead body of their beloved on that first Easter morning. Then the priest led the procession back to the church, mounted its steps and threw open the front doors of the church. It was, like

the tomb, empty. Nothing there! The priest shouted out the ancient paschal
greeting:"Christ is risen."

And the crowd replied,

"He is risen indeed."

My friend told me, by the way, that the chief reason for the police
presence was to prevent people from sneaking into the empty church while
the procession circled the block. I suppose having a full church of trespass-
ers would ruin the dramatic effect of the church as empty tomb. The other
thought I had when I heard this story from my friend was that there is
certainly no need for a police presence to keep people from sneaking into
most of our churches. In fact, I think I would like a few more people, even if,
especially if, they are trespassers.

I was very much struck with the Orthodox custom, which, I learned
later, is by no means confined to Russia. My Greek Orthodox sister-in-
law, for example, knew all about it. So, the following Easter, and many
Easters since, I have used it as the equivalent of a children's story during
morning worship. First, I teach the paschal greeting with the children
saying, "Christ is risen," and the congregation responding, "He is risen
indeed." I then explain the practice to the children and lead them in procession around the outside aisles of the sanctuary. As we walk, I remind
them in subdued and saddened tones of the Good Friday story and tell
them we are going to the tomb to anoint the body of Jesus. There is normally, in most churches, a door into the remainder of the structure, near
the front of the church. (I strongly advise checking out what is behind the
door before opening it. A view of a janitor's bucket and mop does tend to
diminish the credibility of the open door/empty tomb imagery.)

I throw open the door, declare that the crucified one is not there: the
children say, "Christ is risen," and the congregation responds, "He is risen
indeed." This is not as impressive as thousands of Russians on the streets
of St. Petersburg, but for a local church, it's not bad.

Cleopas and Martha

One Easter Sunday morning when our son Allan was a teenager and had
taken on the role of Sunday school teacher, we had a little trouble getting him
to the table in time for a family breakfast suitable to the feast day.

"Sorry," he said, "I was working on my Sunday school lesson." (This is
not his mother's fault. He takes after his father and tends to leave preparation

until the last minute.) I offered a feeble Easter morning joke: "What's the lesson about?"

I would have deserved a smart reply like, "Christmas, of course! What do you think?" Instead, we got a serious response.

"It's about that story in Luke where Jesus appears to the two disciples while they are walking to Emmaus and then has dinner with them. You know, Cleopas and Martha."

"Martha?" said his mother.

"Yes, Cleopas and Martha," reaffirmed Allan.

"There's no Martha in the story. The other disciple, the one with Cleopas, isn't named," we informed him.

"Well, she's Martha in the lesson," Allan insisted.

Now, I think I know why there is a Martha in the lesson. There aren't enough women heroes and characters in the Bible stories for contemporary taste (though the Easter story is an exception to that general rule). It is genuinely important to make women and girls feel included in the story. Why not change a trivial detail and make the other disciple Martha? There is nothing inherently impossible about the idea and, in a way, I think the identification is partially correct. We shrugged and dropped the matter.

But I wondered about the other question; why didn't Luke name the other disciple? There is an easy answer: the name didn't come down in whatever tradition Luke may have used. He didn't know the name. I do not think that answer is sufficient. The more I think about Luke in particular, the more I stand in awe of his surpassing skill as a storyteller. If Luke left out the name, there was a reason for doing so. He didn't leave out the name from ignorance or by accident.

The scientific method of Bible study—looking at how much space the story takes up on a page—demonstrates that the Emmaus Road story is the longest of all the Easter appearance stories. Luke took time to tell the story, probably a sign that he considered it very important. Now, it is not, I think, because he is trying to offer good evidence for the resurrection. Paul is offering evidence in 1 Cor 15:3–8 where he lists the witnesses with Peter first, then the twelve and all the rest. It's good evidence. But the Emmaus Road story is not.

If you doubt that assertion, imagine an attorney cross-examining Cleopas.

"Mr. Cleopas, were you one of the group closest to Jesus, the twelve?"

"Well, no."

"And what time of day was it when the key events happened?"

"It was dusk, as evening was drawing on."

"Dusk, when it is notoriously difficult to see clearly?"

"Yes, it was."

"I see, and you" (consults notes) "recognized him in 'the breaking of the bread?'"

"Yes."

"You are aware that every pious Jewish male breaks bread and blesses God before a meal?"

"Of course."

"And yet that common gesture made you think it was Jesus?"

And so on.

The appearance to the key witness in the Christian tradition, Peter, together with the twelve, occurs offscreen in Luke. No, Luke, the consummate storyteller, is not offering evidence as such. He is doing something else.

Scholars and preachers have long noticed that the hearts of the two disciples "burn within [them]" when the risen Christ interprets the Scriptures to them and points to his presence in and through all the Scriptures. And he is made known to them in the "breaking of the bread." The interpretation of Scripture and the breaking of bread are the kinds of things that can happen in worship and can happen even now.

Luke isn't offering evidence for the resurrection. He is describing the way disciples of any sort can meet the risen Christ even now. And that may be at least as important as evidence. So perhaps the Sunday school lesson did get it right. The other disciple's name could be Martha. But it could be your name also. I think that's the right answer to the identity of the other disciple. It's "Your Name Here."

The Easter Morning Sunrise Service

I admit that the following unedifying little tale may only be appreciated by readers who, like me, are very definitely not morning people.

I had a professor who was famed for his vast knowledge and also for his surpassing grumpiness. In fact, he may have been the grumpiest man in the history of the Presbyterian Church, a title to which there have been many worthy claimants.

According to the story, the professor was asked by an earnest lady to conduct an Easter sunrise service at 5:30 in the morning.

He replied, "Madam, at that hour of the morning I don't even believe in God, let alone want to worship him."

It may not be edifying, but the tale has been very useful to me. I have repeated the story on several occasions in several places, and nobody asks me to attend early morning events anymore. All to the good, I say.

The same professor was similarly tactful with respect to at least one aspect of ecumenism. He is reputed to have declared once in class, "Bishops are an abomination in the eyes of the Lord. At least, they're an abomination in my eyes, so I presume they're an abomination in the eyes of the Lord!" He may not have been the ideal choice if a search committee were seeking an ecumenical officer for a denomination. The professor will reappear later in this chapter.

With respect to Easter, far too many stories and observations appear about new life "springing" forth at the season of new life in nature. Whatever Easter may be, it is not a process within nature such as new shoots of green appearing after a long winter or the emergence of a butterfly from its chrysalis. It is not an event within nature at all, nor is it about the season of the year. When I hear this kind of illustration in a sermon, I begin to parallel my old professor in grumpiness. A good test for the appropriateness of stories and illustrations might be this: Would this story or observation be just as appropriate if I were speaking in Patagonia, where nature is about to enter the depths of winter?

A more edifying and homiletically useful Easter story is "It's Not Over Yet," which may be found near the end of the introduction of this book.

Mother's Day

Here is a guess that is based purely on personal experience and anecdotal evidence: more bad and overly sentimental sermons may have been preached on Mother's Day than on any other day of the year. I think this is because we are tempted on Mother's Day to get our loves out of proportion. As I write this chapter, it happens that my own mother has died very recently at the age of ninety-three, and many stories about her are coming to mind. This is a story I recall about Mom.

How Much Do You Love Me?

One day when I was a small boy I approached my mother and asked, "Mom do you love me the most, more than my brother and sister?" (Self-centered little beggar, wasn't I!)

Mom looked at me very directly and replied, "No, I love God first and then your father and then the three of you children the same."

I am grateful to have been raised by a mother who put things, including love, in the right order.

Pentecost

Pentecost is one occasion when it actually makes sense to use some Hebrew and Greek in our teaching and preaching.

In Hebrew the word for "spirit" is *ruach.* The *ch* is pronounced somewhat as in the name Bach. But *ruach* does not only mean "spirit" but also "breath" and "wind." Read the story in Ezek 37 of the Valley of the Dry Bones with that knowledge in mind. Or, for that matter, think of those multiple possible meanings when reading the story of the first Pentecost in Acts 2. It helps, however, to tell even a brief story to accompany this linguistic instruction.

The Life is in the Breath

I remember when our first son, Allan, was born. He was, as my father-in-law put it, a typical Presbyterian even before birth, stubborn and upright. In more medical terms, he was a breech presentation who never turned, as most babies do, into the head-down position for birth. The medical people in England, where we were living at the time, were willing to consider a vaginal delivery for a breech baby, if all the measurements were favorable, so the relevant tests were undertaken. We had not yet heard the results of the tests when Patty went into a three-weeks-early labor, though the data were on file in an office in the hospital. It was the middle of the night, but the university's professor of obstetrics was awakened and informed of the measurements; then his judgment on the matter was sought. In Allan's case, the professor opined, the measurements were not favorable. A Caesarian section it would be.

At that time, fathers had routinely been allowed to be present in delivery rooms in England, even for C-sections. After the prep work was done, I was masked, gowned and led into the operating theater. They sat me down on a low stool by Patty's head, opposite the anesthetist. A screen, as I was informed ahead of time, had been set up across the mother's chest so that, in theory, the father would be unable to see the surgical opening directly, become distressed and cause a "distraction." (It is interesting to consider what would be a "distraction" in such a case.) In fact, I was so tall that even from a low stool, I could see the business in hand directly over the top of the screen. It was fascinating and, as it turned out, I was in no danger of becoming a distraction.

Finally, after obviously efficient and skilled work by the whole team, the key moment arrived. The surgeon reached into the opening and drew out our son. C-section babies are often very beautiful because their heads are not misshapen after passage through the pressures of the birth canal. So it was with Allan, but even aside from the lovely shape of the head, I thought my newborn son was the most beautiful sight I had ever seen.

Yet he wasn't breathing. My stomach turned. Very calmly, the surgeon handed Allan to a nurse who wrapped him in a blanket and carried him to a small table in the corner of the room. On the table was a cylinder of oxygen and attached to it a tiny mask. The nurse fit the mask over Allan's nose and mouth and turned a valve on the cylinder.

"Pssst, Pssst, Pssst!" I heard. And Allan drew his first breath and there was life.

The Final Breath

I have been present at the other end of life also.

On one occasion I went to the local hospital to visit an elderly gentleman from the congregation who was ill but not thought to be in imminent danger of death. Consequently, no one from the family was present at the bedside. When I arrived at the room, though the door was open, the curtains around the bed had been drawn. I could hear the nurse moving about behind the curtains, so, of course, I waited. Finally, she emerged through the curtain. She gave a start of surprise as she saw me, wearing a clerical collar that explained without words why I was there. (A clerical collar is often useful in pastoral visiting.)

"Oh!" she said. "He just died. Would you like to see him?"

I stepped through the curtain and there was the gentleman. Unlike other deaths for which I had been present, no family members were present to require my pastoral attention, so I could look more closely at the body itself. The man's face was the same as usual. His eyes were still open and he was even still warm. But the breath was gone. Life had departed. What a difference!

Life is in the breath, and the Holy Spirit is the Breath of Life in the church.

Reformation Sunday and All Saints'

In the wider calendar in North America, the last day of October is Halloween, and the following day is chiefly a binge day for candy. In the official church year, the next day is All Saints' Day. In the confused middle, where churches of my tradition tend to live, the custom is often to preach a Reformation-themed sermon on the Sunday nearest to October 31. Such a sermon commemorates the occasion on which Martin Luther nailed his Ninety-Five Theses to the church door in Wittenberg, a good story in itself, but one that historians say may be more true than factual. Whether that is the case or not, we Protestants have our saints' stories also. Reformation Sunday is a good time to tell the Protestant version of saints' stories, and All Saints' Day is a good time to tell some of the wonderful tales of the saints from a wide variety of traditions

I was "traditioned into" the Reformed version of Christianity chiefly by the stories of my church historian father. One of the smaller tasks of the Christian storyteller is to tell again some of the stories that lie at the heart of our particular traditions. The stories at home in all or most our traditions are more important, however. Telling them is a greater task. But even small tasks ought to be done and done well. Here, therefore, are several stories that speak of my own Reformed tradition. The point for members of other traditions is that they too should tell their stories at the appropriate time. If we do not tell the stories, our traditions will likely become bland and banal.

Well, here's a story:

The Heart of Christianity?

There is a story about Ian Pitt-Watson, a great Scottish preacher who was called to Southern California to teach preaching. He was, of course, in immediate demand as a guest preacher in the Presbyterian churches of Southern California—he had a Scottish accent, after all. For six months, however, he refused all invitations, choosing rather to attend different services in a variety of congregations, the better to assess the state of the church in his new home. After six months he announced that he was ready to accept invitations because he now understood the heart of Christianity in those churches: "It's nice to be nice and it's good to be good."

I would not dare say that in our own churches a more profound gospel is always preached and heard.

The Seven Chief Emphases of the Reformed Tradition

There was once a professor of Reformed theology famed both for his learning and for his surpassing grumpiness. Late in his teaching career a certain colleague, the professor of pastoral counselling, as the story has it, became dean of the seminary. The new dean mandated that all assignments and examinations should be based on "real-life" pastoral situations. You can imagine what the grumpy professor thought of this development. Still, Presbyterians are obedient to all lawful authority, so the professor designed a final examination for his introduction to Reformed theology with one question that obeyed the mandate of the dean:

You are a Presbyterian minister and you decide to travel to another city by a late-night bus. In the darkness you mount the bus and make your way to the one vacant seat. You become aware that you are sitting next to a young woman who is weeping bitterly. As a pastor you turn to her and say, "Young woman, I am a Presbyterian minister! How may I help you?"

She replies, "A Presbyterian minister! Oh, thank God! Tell me, I have always wanted to know: what are the seven chief emphases of the Reformed tradition?"

A correct answer to that examination question would include both an emphasis on the preaching of the word and on glorifying God. In this connection some may even remember the first question and answer of the Shorter Catechism: "What is man's chief end? Man's chief end is to glorify God and enjoy him forever."

The Baker of Geneva

There is an old story about John Calvin preaching a sermon in Geneva about glorifying God, a key element of the Reformed tradition. The baker of Geneva was very much taken by the sermon and approached Calvin to ask a key question.

"Master Calvin, how may I glorify God?"

He expected a very spiritual or religious answer, but instead Calvin replied, "Bake good bread."

By the way, I cannot footnote that story. My father used to tell that story, but I have no idea where he found it. I have read a number of books and articles about the great Reformer of Geneva but have never seen a reference to the little tale. I even helped host a conference on Calvin in connection with the five hundredth anniversary of his birth and mentioned the anecdote with the theme speaker. He hadn't heard of the story either, despite having recently published a major biography of Calvin. The story may still be "true," however. It says something true about Calvin, about the Reformed tradition, and probably about my father also. All forms of honest work are a calling from God, and we honor God when we do our work well.

Gas Barbecues and the Law of God

Another distinctive characteristic of the Reformed tradition, of which Presbyterians are a part, is that we think the law of God is mainly a good thing. It is sweeter than honey, a light for our feet and a lamp for our path, as the psalmist would say. Now, we do know that we are not put right by obeying the law of God or, indeed, by any achievement of our own. It is all a gift of free grace on which we lay hold by faith. And, of course, anything, including the law of God, can be misused. But at heart the law remains a blessing.

This is how it is supposed to work. If the love of God actually means anything to us, we will want also to show our gratitude to God. Grace evokes gratitude. We don't want to sink back into a warm bath of piety and do nothing for God or for others. One way to show gratitude is to offer our praise. Another way to show gratitude is to live a life of grateful obedience. The law of God shows us how to do just that.[1]

1. In Reformed theology, this is known as "the third and principal use of the law."

I remember trying to put together a gas barbecue with my father-in-law and a very senior ministerial friend of his. I am not Mr. Fixit, and the other two were . . . well, both have passed on, and it is unseemly to speak ill of the dead. But that wasn't the real problem. When we opened the shipping container, we realized that the main problem was that the instructions were missing. (More exactly, we did have what appeared to be instructions in Chinese, but since none of us could read Chinese, that was less than completely useful.) There were approximately three million moving parts in neat plastic bags in the box, and if you put a gas barbecue together wrongly, the thing might blow up. We tried to put the barbecue together from first principles. Three ministers and a screwdriver. This had the makings of a bad scene from a sitcom.

After about twenty minutes we were in serious danger of doing one another injury with hand tools when my wife burrowed into the box and found, wedged under a flap, the instructions. What a gift! We now had instructions from the Original Equipment Manufacturer showing us how to put this very complicated appliance together. The instructions from the maker were a blessing.

In the Hebrew of the Old Testament, the word that is normally translated as "law" is *torah*. But *torah* could just as easily be translated "instruction." The Maker blesses us with instruction that help us safely put together this very complicated thing called life. Instruction from the Maker is indeed a blessing.

Daniel and the Reindeer Head

When Daniel was a small boy he was a "Beaver." The Beavers are an organization for children, originally boys but now girls also, who are too young to join the Cub Scouts. At the time, Daniel was six years old, if I recall correctly. A few weeks before Christmas, the leaders organized a parent and child evening in which the Beavers and their parents would take on a shared project.

The project, as it turned out, was to create a wooden clothes rack, shaped more or less like the head of a reindeer or perhaps of a moose. A member of the deer family, anyway. This involved cutting from a rectangle of thick plywood the reindeer's head and antlers, and topping things off with a bright red puff of a nose in the middle. (Definitely a reindeer, on second thought!) The child's clothes could then be hung, the leader explained, on the points of the antlers. To my considerable surprise each parent was handed an electric jigsaw. We were informed, furthermore, that we ourselves would not be cutting out the convoluted shape of the reindeer head and antlers. Our job was to give instruction so that the children themselves could do so safely. I had visions of missing fingers on Daniel's much-loved hand so I spoke very firmly.

"You must not let your hand get anywhere near the blade," I said.

"You must not let the cord get anywhere near the blade."

"Thou shalt not put thy hand under the working surface."

"Thou shalt stop immediately if I tell thee to do so."

Moses after a hard day with the Israelites could not have spoken more firmly. Passersby might even have supposed that I spoke harshly, if they missed the love behind the firmness. But Daniel heard the love in the instruction.

"Yes, Dad!" he replied and he positively vibrated with joy and anticipation, for the instruction was making him ready (more ready than his father, to be honest) for something new, exciting, and wonderful.

To be sure, the law sometimes accuses, showing us how short we fall of the will of God, and smashing our pretensions like Luther's bloody great hammer. But it also instructs the redeemed in the art of leading a new and sometimes even wonderful life. The law is not simply a taskmaster but also shapes us (with the Spirit's help, to be sure) for a freedom we could otherwise not know.

By the way, Daniel still has ten fingers.

A Wittenberg Crucifix

Reformation Sunday always reminds me that in the summer of 2007 I was able to visit Wittenberg, Germany, Martin Luther's town. This is the birthplace of the Protestant reformation, where Martin Luther may or may not have hammered the Ninety-Five Theses of revolt against a corrupt Church on the doors of the Castle Church. Though the story about the theses may be apocryphal, it is a more important and unchallengeable fact that there Luther preached the gospel week by week. In the city church of Wittenberg, where Martin Luther usually preached, is an altar, and on the altar a set of paintings by Lucas Cranach the Elder, Luther's friend. The painting below the altar shows the citizens of Wittenberg listening to a preacher. If you look carefully, you can see Cranach himself with his heavy beard. You can see Luther's wife, Katarina von Bora. You can see Luther's little son, Haenchen, whom he loved so dearly, and in the pulpit, quite recognizably Martin Luther himself. Luther's hand is outstretched, and he is pointing to a crucifix—a representation of Jesus Christ hanging on the cross; an image of the son God gave up so that all God's sons and all God's daughters might come home.

My wife, Patty, and I gave a print of that painting to our son Allan, who was ordained to the ministry also in that summer of 2007. We wanted to remind him every day that his task, like Luther's, like that of the church, is always to point to Christ and specifically to Christ on the cross.

I have several friends whose relationships with their children are far more complex and strained than mine are with my sons. The parents will not let those children go, no matter what the children have done. They love them still. That kind of love is closer to God's love than is mine, I think. God will not give up on God's children. The depth of that love is shown in the cross. That is a gospel worth preaching.

Saints

Then there is this business of thinking that the people in our churches, with all their troubles, are saints. I am writing this material from a classically Protestant theological position and must admit that we Protestants don't normally speak or write much about saints. That is a pity in many ways. Among other things, failing to talk about saints cuts us off from a marvelously rich treasury of stories. We ought to be able to tell many stories of saints without having to repeat the more fanciful and absurd tales or surrendering to the kind of commercial activity around the merits of the saints that, among other things, led to the Reformation. The real challenge here, however, is that when Paul speaks that way about the Corinthians, he clearly is not using the word *saint* the same way we generally do.

People the Light Shines Through

There is an old story about a young boy taken for the first time to a Gothic cathedral. He looked up at the stained glass windows, the morning sun blazing through their magnificence, and asked, "Who are those people?"

Told they were "saints," he replied, "Ah, I see. Saints are people the light shines through!"

A Child Who Will Turn Out Well

I remember taking my mother out to lunch one day. As we left the restaurant, we saw a fine little boy, perhaps four years old, standing handsome and neatly dressed by the restroom doors. My mother, who has been partial to little boys for many years now, bent over and said to him, "You're a fine young man, aren't you!"

He looked up at her and confidently replied, "Yes. That's what my mother says, too!"

We sometimes think we are self-created women and men. Even on the purely human level, that is not true. We are very likely to become what the most important people in our lives think we are.

That little boy will very likely turn out well because his mother thinks he is wonderful.

The most important being not just in your life but in the universe looks at you and sees something wonderful. That One sees saints.

Adopted Child

Very few times in parenting is there a completely right answer, but I do know of one. I have been told that in a family with an adopted child as well as biological children, the adopted child will eventually ask the mother whether she loves the adopted child as much as the ones born from her body. There is a right answer to that question. It is this: "Of course I love you. I chose you."

We are saints not because of our own efforts, but because God has loved us and chosen us.

REMEMBRANCE DAY/MEMORIAL DAY

HK

In my first church, back in the early eighties, there was a particular custom on the Sunday nearest to Remembrance Day. Remembrance Day is November 11, the day the guns at last fell silent at the end of World War I. It is the equivalent in Canada and some other parts of the old British Empire of Memorial Day in the United States. Therefore it is very important to Canadians. In my first church, on that Sunday the veterans would act as ushers and wear the blue blazers that are almost a uniform for Canadian veterans, with their decorations, medals, and campaign ribbons. In those days many active members of the church were veterans of World War II. All the veterans deferred, however, to one short and unassuming man named Ron. In addition to the usual decorations of World War II veterans, Ron wore a yellow and red armband adorned with a rising sun and the letters HK.

I had read enough history to know what that meant. "HK" stood for Hong Kong. In late 1941, the British government sent a regiment of inexperienced and ill-equipped Canadian soldiers, largely from Winnipeg, to Hong Kong, then a British colony completely surrounded by Japanese-held territory in China. It was a purely symbolic presence. What could a regiment do against the several divisions of the Japanese Army surrounding the city? But Winston Churchill's attachment to symbolism proved deadly for the garrison. When the war began in the East, soon after their arrival, the defenders resisted as long as they could, losing many lives, but then, inevitably, surrendered. That was the beginning of the horror for the prisoners. Those who know American history might think of the equivalent of the Bataan death march. Many were murdered. Others starved or died of disease or from the brutal treatment they endured as slave laborers. But some survived, sick and emaciated. Ron was among them. No Canadians had a worse war than the Hong Kong Veterans.

Ron was an unassuming man by nature and rarely spoke of these things, though he told me that he had weighed less than a hundred pounds at the end of the war. Eventually, when I had got to know him well enough to speak of his experiences, as I judged, I very tentatively asked him whether he still felt bitter towards the Japanese. This is what he answered and I swear this is both true and factual: "Nah. I like the Japanese. I've been back twice."

That kind of forgiveness and the resulting inner peace is its own kind of victory. No medals are given for such victories, but the victories are real.

6

The Inn: A Story for the Times between Christmas and Easter

This tale began as a story sermon preached on "Low Sunday," the Sunday after Christmas. Perhaps the name Low Sunday refers to the level of spiritual energy in the congregation or simply to the attendance in a typical church. It is also the Sunday when congregational ministers often invite friends who are clergy without churches to fill in for the day because they desperately need a day off after the rush of the Christmas season. So it was that I decided to preach a different sort of a sermon—a story that grew in the first place from the tragic description of the slaughter of the baby boys of Bethlehem, and that led to the continuing story of the gospel. It is an imaginative expansion of a small handful of biblical texts—a pattern followed, to give but two examples, in the ancient tale of Joseph and Aseneth from the first century BCE perhaps, and in many modern tales like and including *The Robe*, by Lloyd Douglas. Soon, however, the tale grew too long for even the most patient of congregations, and I now share it with you in its full-grown form. Still, the story may indicate what may be done on certain Sundays of the year when many congregations are simply ready for a story.

The wind was blowing from the east that day, from the cold desert hills across the Jordan. It was bitter, the east wind, and young Simon had been firmly instructed by his uncle to be sure that the door to the inn stayed closed. The house was full and there was no point in troubling a house full of paying guests simply to lure in those who could not be accommodated anyway. Simon's uncle, the innkeeper, was in his accustomed position behind the bar doling out the red Syrian wine to the company. Simon's mother, newly widowed, nursed Simon's small brother as she prepared the stew for the evening meal. It was good, living in an inn, especially when the travelers told their long tales of distant lands and wonders unknown to tiny Judean villages.

Simon almost missed the first tap on the door, but the second, a more vigorous rap, shook him from his comfortable post. He opened the door a trifle and slipped out into the dust-laden wind. The man was a little below the medium size except in the arms which were long and strongly built. The hands were massive, with heavy calluses and only four fingers on the left hand.

"Carpenter, or perhaps sailor," thought Simon. Simon looked up at the stranger's eyes which were shot with red from the dust and perhaps from something else.

"We need a place to stay," he said.

"The whole town's full," replied Simon. "It's the census, you know."

"I know about the census," answered the stranger, "but they said you might have room. My . . . wife, she . . . " He nodded towards the left. For the first time Simon caught sight of another figure, huddled against the wall for shelter from the biting wind. She was young, far younger than the man, realized Simon. In fact she was not that many years beyond Simon himself. Her belly was stretched like a newly filled wineskin. She raised her head for an instant and Simon was caught by her eyes. There was something about the eyes that made Simon unwilling to add to their troubles.

Simon looked back towards the man, husband rather. "Tie your beast to the post and follow me," instructed Simon as he slipped through the door into the main room of the old inn. Every eye turned toward the three as they entered, even the squint-eyed stranger who had so carefully avoided looking directly at anybody all day.

"Uncle, these people need a place to stay," announced Simon. Uncle wiped his hands on the wine-stained cloth at his waist. His brow furrowed with trouble.

"I truly am sorry," he said, "but the house is full to overflowing. Perhaps you can try one of the homes in the village. They're taking in visitors these days. The census, you know."

"We tried there first," said the traveler. "My wife, she needs privacy just now." All eyes turned to the girl, who bowed her head with shame and embarrassment.

"I see what . . . Well, I would like to help but . . . " Just then Simon's mother swayed through the door from the kitchen, child on hip.

"Surely we can squeeze them in somewhere," she reasoned. "There's a little floor space in the room with . . . " She glanced slightly in the direction of the squint-eyed stranger.

"No, perhaps not there," she sighed.

"I tell you the truth, sir," said uncle. "There's not a cubit's worth of space in the house. Why, there's hardly even space in the stable, let alone . . . "

"Is the stable dry? And out of the wind?" asked the newcomer.

"You seem powerfully eager to find a place in this village," observed Squint-eye, abandoning any attempt to remain inconspicuous. "The government won't worry too much about missing you. Unless you belong to certain families, that is. What's your name, Stranger?"

"Joseph," replied the newcomer.

"Joseph Ben David?" continued Squint-eye.

"Joseph . . . Ben Jacob," came the reply, with a slightly defiant tone to the voice.

"I warrant you're not too happy with the government, making you travel at this time of year. And with her in that condition."

"I say nothing against the government," stated Joseph flatly. "Neither against the Romans nor King Herod."

Simon was surprised that his uncle was allowing the questioning to go on so long, but no one else appeared to share his surprise. The other guests were determinedly studying the quality and clarity of the Syrian wine.

Just then the pregnant girl swayed dizzily. "You poor thing!" exclaimed Simon's mother as she caught the girl's elbow.

"The stable," said Joseph. "It'll have to do for now!"

"Certainly," replied Uncle hurriedly. "Simon, boy, help the lady and her husband."

Simon ran ahead into the dim light of the stable. Swiftly he shifted several of the tired beasts closer together to make space in the corner stall farthest from the east wind. From the byre he brought fresh hay to scatter on the packed earth of the floor. In truth, the stable was not such a bad place after all. Certainly the animals did not reek so strongly as some of the paying guests. Their gentle nickering was softer on the ears than the braying laughter of the drinkers in the bar. "And not nearly so many fleas!" thought Simon. He piled more straw close to the wall.

"That will make not so very bad a bed, sir, ma'am," said Simon. The girl smiled; perhaps it was the first time in her life that anyone had called her ma'am.

"It will do very well, but do not call me ma'am. Simon is it? My name is Mary," replied the girl.

The shed was growing gloomy in the gathering dusk. Simon looked about. "I'll bring an oil lamp," he said. "But I think my mother would say, 'Mind the straw!'"

"So she would, boy," said Joseph as he settled his wife next to the wall.

Simon slipped back to the inn. His mother was stirring the stew, sniffing with complacency the steam rising from the pot. "Take some of this stew to that poor dear and her man," she said to Simon. "And some bread and a small skin of the wine. She needs it by the look of her."

When Simon returned to the stable, burdened with lamp, flask and clay pot of stew, he noticed that Joseph was gently stroking Mary's hand. Silently he laid the provisions beside Joseph and hung the lamp from a protruding nail.

"May the God of Israel bless you for your mercy on the strangers who come to your door!" spoke Joseph. Mary simply opened her eyes and looked her thanks.

"It is little enough," replied Simon, abashed.

"There is nothing little about hospitality," said Joseph.

Simon nodded his amen and went out into the gloom firmly closing the stable door behind him.

The night was long and busy in the inn. Simon could see the smile tugging at the corner of his uncle's mouth as the wine poured out and the coins rolled in. No one spared a thought for the animals in the stable, let alone for the humans there. At last the inn grew silent and Simon lay quietly beside his mother and small brother. He slept deeply, waking but once hearing a slight scuffling in the street and sniffing the unmistakable odor of hill-raised sheep.

"Those dirty shepherds!" muttered his mother. "What are they doing here at this time of year? And all the bars are closed too!" But she tumbled back into sleep and they heard no more until the rooster crowed its welcome to the sun.

It was Simon's daily task to muck out the beasts in the stable. He entered the stable lit by the slanting rays of the morning sun. Joseph stirred and came forward to greet Simon.

"Perhaps you could ask your mother to step out if she is able, young man," said Joseph.

"My mother? She never works the stable, sir," replied Simon.

Joseph beckoned Simon forward with a shrug of the shoulder and a slight motion of the four-fingered hand. Simon stumbled forward three steps, looked around Joseph, and saw, laid in the manger, wrapped tightly in old but clean cloths, a sleeping baby. Mary, whose face seemed as white as the fleece of the sheep on the hills, looked up at Simon. She seemed content.

"What's his name?" asked Simon.

Mary did not answer but looked a question at Joseph.

"I think we had better call him Jesus," answered Joseph. He muttered something under his breath. Simon was not quite sure that he had heard correctly. It sounded like something about "people" and "sins." An odd thing to say about a baby, he thought.

"I'll fetch my mother straightway, sir," said Simon and ran to do so.

Some guests registered for the census early that day and left the dusty village. Uncle managed to find a room for the family in the inn.

"A little late but better than never!" he exclaimed.

That evening Joseph joined the company in the public room. After surveying the crowded bar, he said, "This seems a prosperous place, good host." he said. "Any work in this neighborhood for a master carpenter?"

"Don't want to go back to Galilee, eh?" interjected Squint-eye who seemed to overhear every conversation in the room. "Don't look so surprised; your accent gives you away. Lots of political trouble up there. In hot water with the authorities up north?"

"Not at all, sir, I assure you," replied Joseph with surprising calm.

"Old man, young wife. The neighbors are talking and all that?" leered Squint-eye.

"Something like that," said Joseph and turned away.

Uncle had been fingering his chin thoughtfully. "That wind yesterday damaged the roof. Let's see how you do with that job, and then we'll decide," he said. "All this census business has been good for our pockets. Perhaps there'll be some building around here. Very likely we'll need a room or two more in this very inn!"

By the next day the registration for the census was completed. The out-of-town guests all departed. Even Squint-eye left, though not without a lingering stare at Joseph. When he was well out of earshot, Uncle whispered out of the side of his mouth to Joseph, "Idumaean accent. Herod's country. Government spy?"

Joseph nodded. "I think so. I imagine he's afraid of people like me, descendants of King David. But all I want is to be left in peace—and to get to work on your roof!"

Joseph proved to be a master carpenter indeed. The visitors for the census had left many good coins in the pockets of the villagers, and he found regular work in the village and in the surrounding countryside. Joseph, Mary and the baby moved into a small clay brick house roofed with the newly popular Greek tiles. When he had a moment to spare, Simon would run over to the house to greet Mary and to play with the tiny Jesus. Simon loved to pick up the tiny wooden toys made by Joseph and hold them before the eyes of the delighted baby. Jesus would always smile at Simon. He had such beautiful eyes, thought Simon, so very much his mother's eyes.

That was the year that the two brightest wandering stars came together to make what almost seemed one bright star in the east. Simon loved the stars; an old friend of his uncle's, Reuben, a sailor on the great sea of the west, had instructed him in the ways of the night sky. The sailor had taught him how sailors navigate by the North Star, how most stars are fixed in their places, but how five wander through the sky, now stopping and moving backwards, now plunging ahead in their paths. The Greeks, Simon knew, called them the wanderers.

"What do these movements mean?" Simon had asked.

"I do not know," replied Reuben. "Only the learned and wise understand such things."

It was about this time that strangers from the east came to the village and following them, once again, Squint-eye. The strangers stayed in the inn, of course.

The chief of the strangers spoke to his friends, "This does seem to be the place. Both the motion of the stars and what we have heard in the City tell us that."

He looked about with an air of slight surprise and addressed Uncle, "So this . . . place is the ancestral home of the great King?"

"That it is sir, and right proud of it we are!"

"And the people here are his descendants?"

"Bless you no, sir, though the Holy One, blessed be He, knows that the great king left enough of them. Why, when the census required them to register here, there wasn't a room to be had in the entire village."

"But you say they have left now? All of them?"

"Well," Uncle said in a low voice, for Squint-eye was not far distant. "There is Joseph and his wife and new baby; they stayed on here. But don't get him into trouble, sir. He's a good fellow and a fine worker."

"I have no intention of getting him into trouble and still less his child. A son, you said?"

"I didn't say, sir. But since you mention it, a son it was. But be careful sir! These things should not be spoken of lightly!"

"We have had only the warmest of welcomes and the most eager assistance since coming to your country. Why this caution?"

"I can tell you are a learned man, sir. Surely you have learned that though the world of nature is plain and trustworthy, it is not so with the world of humans." Here Uncle dropped his voice further, "Or of Kings."

The stranger asked no more but quietly sipped his wine. Later that evening, he took Simon by the arm and asked, "Boy, can you direct me to the dwelling of this Joseph of whom your Uncle has spoken?"

"I can, sir. Indeed, I can take you there in less time than it would take to give you the directions."

The strangers followed Simon through the winding streets. When they reached Joseph's tiny house, they paused before the door. The youngest of the strangers was carrying a small but richly carved chest. "Here?" he asked with surprise.

The chief looked to the sky, nodded gently and said, "The ways of the Mighty One are strange indeed. But have we not been guided? Boy, we thank you for your part in the guiding. You may go to your home now."

Simon knew that this last word was not permission but command. He returned to the inn.

The next morning Joseph came to visit Uncle. It was so early that the guests were yet asleep, even Squint-eye. Joseph's brow was furrowed and his voice anxious.

"I thank you for your kindness to me and to my family, but I must leave this place. I fear I must ask you for the last of my wages."

"Certainly, Joseph. I would not for a minute hold back your wages, but why this sudden decision?"

"I cannot truly say, but I know that there is great trouble coming. I do not know how or why, but great sorrow is drawing near. I urge you to send away those whom you love."

"Well, Joseph, to my mind one place is very much like another in this troubled world. And times have never been so good in Bethlehem. I think we'll stay. But where will you go? Back to Galilee?"

"No," replied Joseph, "not there. Perhaps we shall travel on to Egypt. There are many of our people in the great city of Alexandria. I can find work for my hands and safety for my family there. But please, tell no one of our plans. We leave immediately."

Simon held the infant while Mary and Joseph packed their few belongings. Before the sun was halfway to the zenith, all was ready.

"I will never forget you," said Simon to the baby, but the infant, as is the way with the very young, said nothing but only looked at Simon with his fine eyes.

"Simon," said Joseph, "Check that no one is about, particularly the gentleman with the squint." The street was quiet, and Squint-eye was in close attendance on the wise strangers. And Joseph and Mary and the child slipped away on the road to the south.

Later that day, the learned strangers also rode away but not northwards towards the City, the direction from which they had come. Rather they traveled directly east towards the great salt sea.

"Odd," said Uncle, "Surely they cannot expect to be taken in by the Essenes. They would not welcome Gentiles. But perhaps they hope to travel by Jericho."

Squint-eye watched the travelers as far as eye could see. He turned to Uncle and said, "Your guests are leaving you. Perhaps it is the quality of your wine!"

"You do not seem troubled by the quality," replied Uncle.

Squint-eye sneered. "Speaking of travelers, where is that Joseph fellow?" But Uncle only shrugged in reply and continued to rotate his barrels of new wine. That night Squint-eye too left the village. He journeyed north, towards the City.

"Good riddance!" said Uncle to his departing figure as it crested the hill to the north.

It was two days later that the soldiers came. Like the locusts of the old stories they descended on the village. With their captain rode Squint-eye. But locusts would have been less cruel. Every baby boy in the village, slaughtered. They seized Simon's small brother from his mother's arms. She turned to Squint-eye calling for mercy, but with a practiced stroke a soldier murdered the child, as coolly as a priest offering sacrifice in the Temple.

Simon's mother flew at the soldiers, arms upraised but he turned and with equal lack of emotion struck her down.

"Run, boy!" shouted Uncle and grappled with the bloodstained sol-der. Squint-eye plunged his dagger into uncle's back. Uncle dropped to the ground, coughing blood.

"That's for the bad wine, old man!" he sneered.

Simon had turned to run but Squint-eye was as quick as he was cruel.

"Get that boy!" he shouted and a guard grasped Simon by the edge of the tunic and hauled him back.

The captain of the troop looked down at Simon. "This one's well over two," he said to Squint-eye. "Only the boys under two. Those were the orders."

"Growing merciful in your old age?" sneered Squint-eye. "They won't like that in the City. Besides, I need information from the shaver. Boy!" he hissed to Simon with a smile as cruel as sudden death. "Show me where that Galilean and his brat are staying, and you'll live."

"But they're gone, sir!" screamed Simon. The smile disappeared.

"If you're lying, boy, you'll live long enough to regret it, but not much longer."

"It's true; I'll show you where they lived, and you can judge for yourself."

Squint-eye shook Simon by the hair and cuffed him on the ear. "No tricks now! Take me there."

Simon led the small party of soldiers through the alleys to Joseph's house. As he had said, the cottage was abandoned. Squint-eye bent down to the hearth and felt among the ashes. "Cold!" he squawked. "Maybe the boy's telling the truth. Keep searching!" He shouted to the soldiers, "I want that Galilean brat!"

He turned back to Simon. "So they left, did they? Back to Galilee, I warrant. Well, that'll do them little good. Boy, which way did your friends go?"

"Not my friends, sir. And I don't know which way they went." But very carefully Simon let his eyes slip slightly toward the north.

"Oh that's how it is, is it?" Squint-eye laughed sneeringly. "Don't try to match wits with your betters, boy. You've told me all I need."

He cuffed Simon again, knocking him spinning against the doorpost. "Now get back to the inn where you belong. There's going to be an opening for an innkeeper in this village, I fancy. And remember, I know where to find you."

Simon stumbled back through the alleys to the ruins of the inn. His uncle, supported by a weeping neighbor, was still breathing, though his shallow gasps told even Simon that death was very near.

"Bend down your ear, Simon," he wheezed. "I'll pass soon. Must tell you . . . coins behind the second last large wine cask. Take them and flee. They'll return for you. Do not lose a moment. Nothing for you here now. You'll never be safe here. Remember my friend Reuben . . . sea captain. He'll care for you, for my sake." Uncle tried to raise his right hand, "The blessing of the God of Abra—" But he never did complete the blessing.

Simon retrieved his old dark cloak, stooped to pick up a loaf still warm from his mother's oven, and bent to grope behind the second wine cask. He felt a small but heavy bag and fetched it out with the aid of a kitchen spoon. He counted out ten coins from the sack to the neighbor and said, "Take this, good friend, and see that my kin are properly buried, I pray you. I must obey my uncle's last command."

By nightfall Simon too had left Bethlehem, traversing by starlight the hill paths westward to the great sea. He reached the port of Caesarea Maritima in three days. By the mercy of God, Reuben's ship was moored a stone's throw offshore. Simon, who could not swim, hired a small craft to row him to the ship. Reuben recognized the exhausted lad from a distance, aided him to scramble up the merchant vessel's inward sloping hull, and took him below to the one great cabin where all the crew slept. When Simon recounted the events in Bethlehem, Reuben wailed and tore his garments. He bent over the cook's hearth, grasped a handful of ashes, and poured it over his head.

"Come with me. Be my cabin boy and also my son!" he cried out. So Simon, the innkeeper's nephew, became a sailor.

The years passed. Simon, no longer the cabin boy, had never grown beyond the middle height, but the years of hauling on ship's lines and wrestling with the great sweep oar rudder had broadened his shoulders and filled out his chest. Few drinkers in the waterfront inns frequented by sailors would dare to challenge his massive strength. Not that Simon sought trouble; he had, he often said, seen enough trouble and cruelty to last a lifetime. With his sturdy frame and corded muscles he could have made a name for himself in the fights that broke out in the sailors' quarters of the port cities, but he avoided trouble rather than seeking it out. In the fullness of time, Reuben chose to rest from his seafaring, and Simon, with the coins saved from his uncle, bought the ship. As captain, he was famed, not only for his great strength, but for his gentleness. The only thing that ever roused him to anger was any sort of cruelty. He took his ship into the lucrative trade in grain between North Africa and Rome, and he prospered.

But Simon was alone. There are men, and many of them are sailors, who have been created by the Mighty One for aloneness. They wander the earth and the seas also, never mooring long in any haven, and never linking their lives to any person. Simon was alone, but he was never made for aloneness. Wherever he sailed he sought out his own people, worshiping in the synagogues, though the righteous scorned him, for as he was a sailor he could not fully keep the Sabbath laws. He found a warmer welcome in the few inns kept by his compatriots.

There was an inn he favored in the grain port of Cyrene. There he took his ease between voyages, sipping slowly at his wine mixed with water. The innkeeper had two daughters, and the younger, thought Simon, was as great an attraction to lonely sailors as the wine. The younger daughter was named Rachel and was as lovely, all considered, as her remote ancestor. Her older sister was named Leah. It was said that her father had given her that name when she came twisted from her mother's womb. A cruel naming it was, thought Simon, but a truthful one. For all loved Rachel, but Leah was disregarded.

One dark evening as Rachel laughed and flirted by the bar with the handsome young merchants from the city, Leah served the more humble customers in the common room, sailors and travelers of every sort. Simon was seated there and near him two sailors from the western coasts. They were well into their cups, he could tell. Still, after the custom of their kind, they called to Leah for more.

When she leaned over the table the one seated nearest to Simon grasped her roughly by her twisted thigh, just where it joined a surprisingly well-rounded hip.

"Give us a squeeze, sweetie," he leered. Her sister Rachel was well used to such advances and always twisted lightly through drunken attempts to grapple. Leah, it was clear, was neither so agile nor so accustomed to such approaches. "Please, sir, let me go!" she cried.

The other sailor groped forward also. "Listen, sweetie, a girl that looks like you can't be choosy. You ought to be glad that real men like us even want to touch you!" He reached forward to stroke her long, dark hair. Leah turned from his reaching hand; her face was now fully visible to Simon. There were tears welling up under the dark lashes. The words, it appeared, were more cruel than the groping hands. For the briefest of moments Leah's eyes met Simon's, then she turned still farther from him in her shame. With grace born of a thousand storm-tossed nights on the great sea, Simon slipped forward. He grasped the offending arms by the wrists and slowly, irresistibly bent the arms backward. The owner of the arms struggled briefly then flopped backward on the bench, unable to move.

"You are troubling this lady. I take it you want to apologize and return to your ship to sleep it off. Nod, if that's what you mean." A slightly increased pressure on the captive arms produced the nod. Simon released the arms and the sailors almost tumbled over one another in their haste to get out of the inn.

Leah turned to Simon, "Thank you, sir," she said. "You can't know what we folk who work in inns have to endure at times." She blinked the tears out of her eyes and smiled gently at Simon. Very fine eyes they were, thought Simon, now that he saw them more clearly. Strange that he had never noticed those eyes before.

"In truth, I do know what inn folk suffer. I grew up in an inn back in Judea," he said.

"Indeed sir? I had thought you were always a sailor. The word goes round that you are a good captain to sail with. Perhaps you would tell me one day how a boy from a Judean inn became a seafarer? When you have the chance, that is. But I mustn't keep you and the others are calling for their wine."

All that evening Simon watched not Rachel but Leah. As he watched, he marveled at the quickness and grace with which, despite her twisted hip and damaged leg, she moved among the tables, laden though she always was with food and drink. "Like a seaworthy vessel for those with eyes to see," he thought. A verse from the Writings came to his mind:

Three things are too wonderful for me,
    four I do not understand:
        the way of an eagle in the sky,
        The way of a serpent on a rock,
        the way of a ship on the high seas,
        and the way of a man with a maiden.

"Now why did I think of that just now?" Simon wondered.

As the inn grew quiet, he beckoned her to sit down next to him and, for the first time in many years began to tell his story. In truth, for a lonely man there is little that is more winning than a woman who listens not just with her ears but with her eyes also, for the eyes are the windows of the soul. The story was too long for one evening's telling, so Simon returned for another.

On the third they spoke of other things. And on the fourth, Simon spoke to Leah's father.

"You want Leah?" said her father. "You mean Rachel, don't you? I always thought I would have to pay a man to take Leah off my hands, but you actually want her?"

Leah listened with head bowed and eyes clouded again with tears.

"Sir, I would not take the smallest coin from you. Indeed, I would gladly give all I have for a wife such as Leah, worthy of a patriarch in Israel, let alone a poor sailor."

"Poor? But I thought . . . "

"He has more than enough, Father. And more than I could ever ask." replied Leah, looking only to Simon.

And so it was agreed. Simon took Leah away from the inn, though often she returned to help her father in the busy times. In the course of time Leah conceived and while Simon was afloat somewhere south of Sicily, bore him a fine son. It was a mighty struggle for her, for the child, it was plain to see, would have his father's frame. When the midwife held the newborn child to her cheek the boy clenched his tiny fist and shook it at the world.

"See the little conqueror!" said the midwife. So Leah named the child Alexander, for Simon was not present to exercise a father's right of naming. Leah's father was pleased with Leah, the more that Rachel, now married also, had born only a daughter.

"A fine son you bear to me! Perhaps you are worth something after all!" shouted the old innkeeper in his glee. When the words were told to Simon on his return, he was displeased. Nevertheless he loved the child, and for his sake and for Leah's also, spoke no word of reproach to his father-in-law.

When Alexander was a small boy, running about the home with wooden sword and threatening wars of conquest against the neighboring cats and dogs, Leah conceived again. By now, Simon owned several ships and did not always voyage with his vessels. He was present for the birth, if it can be said that a man is present for such things, for the midwife and the other old women drove him from his own house. "We will call you when it is necessary," they said.

The women did not call him until night had drawn on, though the pains had grasped Leah at the dawn of the day. "You have a second fine son," said the midwife, touching Simon's forearm gently. "But it has been too much for Leah. She cannot live long."

Simon bent over the low bed where Leah lay. She was white, as white as the clouds over the great sea on a fine summer's day, and her breath was as quiet as the land breeze on a still morning. He could not speak for the tears were flowing backward into his throat. Leah opened her fine eyes and whispered to her husband, "Do not let my Father have the boys while you are at sea. Care for them yourself. And, I thank you. Thank you for it all." And her eyes closed and she was at rest.

Simon named their son Reuben, for he remembered his old master and also the words of the ancestor Leah in the Torah. "Perhaps the Lord will look on my affliction and be merciful," he said. But Reuben was red of hair and skin, so the neighbors all called him not Reuben but Rufus.

The last words of his wife troubled Simon greatly, for he too did not want to leave his sons to be reared by their grandfather, but how was a sailor to watch over small children? In the end he spoke to his father-in-law.

"When a man grows older, he begins to think again of the land of his youth. I have said 'Next year in Jerusalem!' too often. I will take my sons and return to Judea. I will sell my ships and take up your trade, the trade of my youth also. I will keep an inn and care for my sons as they grow."

The old man grew pale when he heard the news. "It will be a hard thing for me to miss my grandsons," he said. "But they are your sons and Leah's also. You must do what seems right in your eyes." He rummaged behind a wine cask and withdrew a surprisingly heavy sack. "But take this gift, for the boys, for you refused any bride money from me. And with it take my blessing, for my grandsons and for you also."

So, when it was safe for the newborn to travel, they parted, more at peace than Simon had dared expect. He did not fear trouble when he reached Jerusalem, for King Herod was long dead and the Romans now ruled directly rather than merely through a local representative. He consulted those who knew the country round about, asking where he could purchase an inn.

"Any little place, not too far from Jerusalem," he said, "But not Bethlehem." When pressed for a reason, he simply replied, "Too many memories."

A sufficient supply of money ensures that such demands are easily met, and within the month Simon and his sons were settled in a village less than a day's walk from Jerusalem. The land was more peaceful under Rome than under Herod, though the taxes were onerous and the Zealots always threatened an outbreak. But the troublemakers, respectful of Simon's sea-hardened limbs, stayed away from Simon's establishment, and it became a favorite stopping place for the quieter sort of traveler. The boys grew straight and healthy, with promise of their father's strength and, from their earliest years, their mother's gentle eyes.

The inn was a bustling place at Passover time when so many of the people of God wished to remember their ancient salvation from Egypt within the bounds of the holy city of Jerusalem. One year so great was the crush in Simon's hostelry that he feared that he would run out of wine for his guests. It was the sixth day and little time was left before the beginning of the Sabbath. Simon decided that nothing else could be done except to go to Jerusalem to arrange for a fresh supply of wine. His business done and the shipment arranged to the satisfaction of Simon and his supplier, Simon strolled in the direction of the temple mount. As he made his way through the festival crowds, he heard a hubbub ahead.

"Make way! Make way!" shouted a guard in Latin-accented Aramaic. "Never stand in the way of Roman law, or it will be the worse for you."

Simon was pressed by the crush of the crowd against the clay brick wall of a harness and leather shop. Though he had no wish to see yet more cruelty, the density of the crowd made escape impossible. He witnessed, unwillingly, a squad of leather-clad Roman soldiers, executioners rather, driving three condemned criminals before them. As was the custom, the three were each carrying a patibulum, the rough and heavy cross timber that would be hoisted into place on the upright. The third poor chap was struggling dreadfully under the weight. For some reason, a circlet of thorns had been thrust down on his head and he was wearing the remains of a robe that looked for all the world as if it were royal purple. It was apparent that he had been savagely beaten; the wounds of the many tails of a Roman scourge marked his back. As Simon watched, the criminal fell, only to be booted to his feet with the thud of heavy army sandals. But he could not stand long under the weight. In the road opposite Simon he staggered again and fell face down on the cobblestones. Again the boot went in, but it was apparent, even to the guards, that this time the condemned would not be able to rise again.

The sergeant of the guard looked about and caught the eye of Simon. For the briefest of seconds he appraised the breadth of Simon's shoulders. "You there!" he shouted, "Pick up this cross."

A murmur arose amidst the crowd. "He's a respectable sort. To be made to carry a criminal's cross. Shame!" the voices said. The sergeant hesitated. It was true that he had been ordered not to cause unnecessary offense, especially during the feast days when feelings always ran high against Rome. The centurion would not thank him if he caused a riot. It was whispered in the barracks that even Pilate himself was eager not to offend the bloody Jews, not since that last protest almost got him removed from office. It was very likely that the sergeant would not have pressed the issue, but by then Simon had bent down and caught sight of the eyes of the condemned man. There was something about those eyes, Simon thought. Then, to his utter amazement the criminal smiled into Simon's eyes. Without a further thought Simon bent down and heaved the patibulum to his shoulders.

Though still a strong man, Simon was no longer young, and the sea muscles had been softened by the easy life of the inn. Simon staggered and his breath was drawn out of him in rending gasps. The last uphill climb to the place called the Skull blurred his mind and all but blinded his vision. "Down here, fellow," came the clipped voice of an officer, and the crosspiece slipped from Simon's weary grasp. Simon stooped, hands on knees, waiting for his breathing to slow and his vision to clear. When he looked up, he saw before his eyes a neighbor from his village.

"What in heaven's name are you doing with that cross, Simon?" asked the friend.

"They made me," croaked Simon when he could speak. "Why are you here?"

"That one robbed and beat my old mother," he replied, indicating the criminal on the left. "I'm here to see that he pays for his sins."

Meanwhile, the guards, practiced and efficient, had hoisted the first two criminals into their places and had laid the third, the one whom Simon had helped, on the patibulum. Simon looked away but he could not avoid the sound of the hammers. In a twinkling they had run a line over the top of the upright, which had remained fixed in place, and were hoisting the heavy laden patibulum into place. No sound came from the criminal, except a long, shuddering intake of breath. The officer in charge handed a crudely lettered placard to a guard, who nailed it to the cross. "Jesus of Nazareth, King of the Jews," it read.

"Political affair, this," remarked the villager. "Ever heard of him?"

"Heard of him, like everybody else, but never paid much attention," replied Simon. "The only Jesus I ever knew personally was taken to Egypt years ago when I was a kid."

But the two villagers were not the only ones to notice the sign. An old man clad gorgeously in the livery of the temple but with a terrible squint in one eye bustled angrily to the officer. "That sign's not right! You need to change the wording."

The officer shrugged. "Orders."

"We'll see about that. My master will speak to Pilate about it. You can be sure of that!"

The officer merely shrugged again, muttered, "Whatever you like," and turned away. The richly dressed old man paused, speechless, then hurried down the hill in the direction of the temple. Only a few women—one, the eldest, supported by a young man with strange, dreamy eyes—were left by the foot of the cross. Simon remembered his duties.

"Must be going," he said. "I don't like this sort of thing. Never have. Not for any of them." With a last glance at the face of the political one, he turned for home. "No smile now," he thought soberly.

The next day, Simon's companion at the place of the Skull came into the inn after the synagogue service.

"Did you stay to the end?" Simon asked. It is, after all an innkeeper's duty as a host to foster conversation on the affairs of the day.

"Yes. It didn't last as long as usual this time. They broke the legs of my fellow and the other thief to put them away before the Sabbath began. That Jesus chap was dead already. I suppose he couldn't last very long after the beating they gave him, but they stuck a spear in him to make sure."

"Poor fellow!" Simon replied gently.

But life was too busy in the aftermath of the festival to worry about Roman justice or anything else except ensuring that the wine kept flowing for the pilgrims making their way home after the Passover.

It was evening the next day, the first day of the week, before Simon could pause to draw a breath. He leaned against the doorpost of his inn and admired the sunset. "Nothing like the sunsets over the great sea though!" he thought.

Three men were walking towards the inn. Simon recognized one as an occasional patron, though he could not at the moment recall his name. The man in the center, hooded and indistinct in the gathering dusk, appeared intent on walking farther before nightfall, but Simon's customer had grasped him by the elbow and was pointing to the inn. With some reluctance, the hooded man gave way and the three made their way toward the inn. Simon retreated to his usual post behind the bar and beyond a slight nod of recognition did not trouble the three, who, it appeared, were continuing a lively conversation.

The three took their places, as so many had before at the innkeeper's table. At length the customer—what was his name?—signaled to Simon for bread and wine, and Simon readily obliged. The hooded stranger pushed back his head covering, broke the bread, held it out to his neighbors and pronounced the ancient prayer, "Blessed art thou, Lord our God, King of the universe, who givest us bread from the ground." The other two guests fell back on their benches as if paralyzed with astonishment. The one who prayed glanced at them fallen back with mouths agape, rose and walked quietly toward the door. As he passed Simon's station, he paused, turned to Simon and said, "Yet one more time will you see me." Simon looked up from his casks. He saw a face marked with a ring of scars about the brows; he looked into the stranger's eyes and realized that the eyes knew him well. And that he knew the eyes also—from Friday, from his youth.

"It's you!" he whispered in amazement.

The figure did not linger, but turned and slipped through the open door into the springtime darkness. Suddenly, the remaining two at their table awoke as from a marvelous dream.

"It was he, here in Emmaus!" they said to one another "Did you see him too? Do you know who he is?" they asked Simon.

"I did and I do," he whispered in return.

But they did not wait to hear the reply; they tossed a pair of coins to Simon and burst out the door in the direction of Jerusalem.

"Yet one more time?" thought Simon. "I will wait. I will wait . . . Master."

And Simon did wait. With every new guest who drew near the inn, he wondered, "Is this the one?" Sometimes when a pious guest broke bread and intoned the ancient prayers, his breath caught in his throat and his stomach quivered, but it was never the one. While Simon waited, the boys grew strong and tall. They became followers of the Way, and, like their father, great travelers. They were not sailors, however, but preachers of the word of Messiah Jesus. And still Simon waited. As he waited the once strong limbs grew ever more feeble, and the voice that had shouted commands against gales on the great sea dwindled to a hoarse whisper. All that remained strong in Simon was an inalterable conviction. "He promised!" he would say to himself, "Yet once more!"

In the end Simon could not even lift his own head from the pillow of his straw bed but had to be cradled in the arms of a maidservant to sip his nourishment. By then the kindly neighbors had sent word to Alexander and to Rufus. They returned before the end and held their father's withered hands. The brothers watched and listened as the now sunken chest lifted for its last time, and they mourned. But there was one strange thing, they recalled as they sat through the traditional days of mourning for their father. Just at the end, at the very moment Simon drew his last breath, his eyes opened one last time, almost, his sons agreed, as if in greeting.

7

Church Life Stories

A Minister's Photo

I was once invited to preach the 175th-anniversary service of a church in a small city east of Toronto. I was welcomed into the church on my arrival by an elder and was ushered down a long corridor towards the minister's study to await the beginning of the service. The corridor was lined with a "rogues' gallery" of photos of former ministers of the church, and I slowed down to look at these representations of the church's past.

My hosts noticed my interest and pointed out one of the earliest examples, a photo of the minister who had served, if I recall correctly, in the late 1840s and 1850s and had died about 1860. "Does that photo look a little peculiar to you?" they asked.

Indeed it did look more than a little peculiar. In fact, it looked almost as bad as the photo on my driver's license.

According to the story they told me, the minister's wife was fascinated by the then very new technology of photography and urged her husband to have his photo made. Whether from theological conviction or from sheer contrariness, a disposition not unknown among us Presbyterians, he steadfastly refused. I can almost hear him say in my imagination, likely in a Scottish accent so typical of many early Presbyterians, "Vanity! Quite possibly idolatry! Thou shalt not make unto thyself any graven image." And he refused.

Then, in about the year 1860, the minister was working in his garden, suffered a stroke, and died . Instead of calling for a doctor, his wife dragged him into the house, dressed him up in his ministerial vestments, propped him up in a chair—and called the photographer.

Of course it looked peculiar!

I have never known what moral to draw from this little tale beyond the truth that the wives of Presbyterian ministers usually get their way in the long run. But there is this thought: "All dressed up for church, and no life." In church this is what we are looking for: we are looking for signs of life, new life.

The Bird

I was a guest preacher in another church in an Ontario city, once again an older congregation, and this time in the absence of the regular minister. Though the building was quite lovely in its nineteenth-century architecture, this church suffered from its location, which meant that it had available the grand total of three parking spaces. One of these was reserved for the minister, who gave me very precise directions on how to find the space. I gave myself time to get lost, but the directions were both accurate and easy to follow. (This is not a common experience for guest preachers. Praise the Lord for the invention of the GPS!) As I traveled, I think I must have prayed for a special anointing that day.

As a result of the excellent directions, I arrived in very good time, and though the church's doors were open, it appeared that no one was there. I parked in the designated spot and climbed out of my car. Above the car were the spreading branches of a gorgeous tree, one perhaps as old as the church building itself. In that tree was a bird. I know this because, as I climbed out of the car, a disturbingly warm substance the consistency but not the smell of thick warm cream spread over the top of my head. I knew immediately what it was and kept my head rigidly still and upright so it would not flow down onto my suit. I walked into the church with the upright posture of a well-trained model on the catwalk and shortly found myself face to face with the duty elder. He approached me with right hand extended and a warm, welcoming smile on his face. The smile faded to a look of horror as he realized what was on the top of my head. I said, "Can you direct me to the men's room?" Without a word, the extended right arm shifted until he pointed down a hallway to his right. There I found sufficient paper towels and managed to clean off my head. There are times when it is an advantage to be bald.

Lord's Supper Disaster

Odd things still happen in church. For example . . .

A young man received his first call as associate minister of a fair-sized church. It turned out that one of his first duties was to prepare the elements for an upcoming communion service. On Saturday evening in the church kitchen, he cut up the bread into dice-sized pieces, spread them on a tray, covered the tray in wax paper, and stuck it in the fridge. Then he looked high and low through the kitchen cupboards for the grape juice but couldn't locate any. Eventually he did find a bag with purple crystals that tasted like grape. He mixed the crystals with water until the mixture tasted about right, poured the juice into the church's little Protestant cups, and placed it all carefully into the refrigerator. The next day was communion; the minister lifted the bread and proclaimed "This is my body." Then he lifted the cup saying, "This cup is the new covenant in my blood . . . "

And the congregation raised their little cups to find . . . Jell-O!

Neither Miracles nor Popcorn

A few years ago I flew from Vancouver to the northern British Columbia town of Kitimat for a speaking engagement, or to be more exact, three speaking engagements. Kitimat is a smelting and pulp and paper-manufacturing town located at the head of a fiord not far south of the Alaska Panhandle. It is situated in a bowl in the midst of what are still, even in May, snowcapped peaks. In former days it had been accessible only by seaplane, but a fine road now links it to Terrace, where the regional airport is located. When founded, Kitimat had been expected to grow to a population of fifty thousand, but for various reasons it stalled at about twelve thousand. That means, of course, that the churches founded in the era of high expectations have never truly flourished either. Still, there are several churches in town, including a small Presbyterian congregation where I would preach on Sunday morning. The fact that the churches are small and in some cases cannot afford regular or full-time ministry means that they cooperate with one another. They also arranged for me to lead a workshop on preaching for all the churches in town.

One of the churches is a fervently evangelistic independent congregation that met for worship on Saturday evening. It was not the kind of congregation that, in my experience, would normally consider inviting as a preacher a professor from a seminary with a rather liberal reputation, as was the case at the time for the school where I was teaching. But in that town, with that cross-denominational willingness to cooperate, sometimes called charity, it was at least possible for this to take place. But possible was as far as it would go, not from ill will, but because the pastor was very eager to have the congregation experience the live broadcast of a "Miracle Crusade" from, as I recall, Florida. Still, the pastor was willing to fit me into the service, if things worked out. "Show up for worship and we'll see," he told me.

The church had purchased the old movie theater in town, complete with plush folding theater seats, projector, and screen, which was already show-ing the Miracle Crusade when I arrived. To top things off, as far as I was concerned, in the lobby there was a still functional popcorn machine. The popcorn machine was in use, and visitors to church could pick up a bag of fresh movie-theater-style popcorn to take into worship. The aroma of fresh popcorn is what I call a welcome.

The theater-become-church also still had its marquee. On the marquee appeared the words "Miracles and Free Popcorn!"

It would be easy for a "mainline" church guy like me to mock a church like this, but I thought to myself, Most of our churches offer nei-ther miracles nor popcorn.

I never was invited to speak there, by the way. I enjoyed the Miracle Crusade and a bag of popcorn for a couple hours and then walked back to my motel for a good night's sleep.

Shaking Hands at the Church Door

People sometimes say strange things to the preacher at the church door. Here's my favorite:

I had preached what I thought was an effective sermon in a church. An older gentleman approached me to shake my hand after the service. It looked as if he shared my opinion about the sermon because on his face was a beam-ing smile. Moreover, he extended to me that two-handed shake—his right hand in mine, his left squeezing the joined hands—that normally indicates warm friendliness. With tremendous enthusiasm in his voice, he looked me in the eye and said,

"All the great preachers are dead!"

How do you respond to that one? I also had a man tell me very warmly, "I like a man who can sell." Hmm. I'm not sure I like that one.

A classmate of mine served her intern year of pastoral experience in a cathedral-sized West Virginia church. After my classmate took part in the service, an elderly lady from the church approached her and said,

"My dear, you do look nice from a distance."

Another friend received a comment I deeply envy. It came from a roughly clad man who shook hands warmly and said, "Freaking good sermon, Reverend!" Only, the man didn't say "freaking."

I think that compliment was one of the most sincere comments possible, if a little unusual in phrasing. You know that, unlike many more conventionally polite churchgoers, he meant what he was saying.

"You Yankees"

But here is the only time I ever actually got in the last word at the church door.

Many years ago I was a student at Union Theological Seminary in Richmond, Virginia, as it was then called. (I mean the seminary, not the city. To the best of my knowledge, the city still bears the same name!) I helped pay for my education by preaching whenever I had the opportunity, mostly in small churches in rural Virginia. All this was quite an experience for a young man from Canada. In one such church there was lady for whom the late unpleasantness between the States or, as she would probably prefer to call it, the War of Northern Aggression, was a living and present reality. She approached me at the door with a sour and jaundiced look on her face as if she wanted to say something nasty to me but could not quite find the right words. I had, I think, preached quite well, at least for a student, so criticizing the sermon was apparently not a possibility. So she chose the next best option for her purposes, namely, reluctant praise. She had noted my accent, which demonstrated that I was certainly not Dixie born and bred, and made a certain assumption about me.

"You Yankees are all so eloquent," she sneered.

I drew myself up to my full height (which is considerable) and replied, "Madam, I'll have you know I am not a Yankee. I am a southern Canadian!"

She had the grace to laugh, and we got along much better after that.

Descent into Hell

Those same rural Presbyterian churches generally recited the Apostles' Creed every Sunday, but many of them, I was told, refused as a matter of conscience to say, "He descended into hell." The organizer of Sunday preaching for students instructed us always to check before the service whether or not that particular church included that line from the creed. One Sunday I forgot to ask. At the appointed time in the service, I stood up and led the congregation through the Creed. They joined me in fine collective voice, all the way through "crucified, dead, and buried." I continued, "He descended into hell." Dead silence. I looked around, drew my breath, and started again, "The third day he rose again from the dead." The congregation joined in as if nothing had happened and accompanied me to the end. I finished the service and took the preacher's usual place at the door ready to shake hands. An elderly lady came up to me, took me by the hand, and announced in a firm voice, "Young man, I think you should know, we don't descend into hell here!"

Hell is a Bad Place to Be

Maybe they don't descend into hell in that church, but lots of people do, in an entirely different and more painful sense.

Together with another minister, named Bob, I was co-interim moderator (Presbyterian for fill-in minister who helps the church find a new pastor) in what is usually called a "vacant church," near Vancouver. ("Vacant church" is an odd phrase, isn't it? Taken literally, it sounds as if the place has been abandoned by all and sundry. But it isn't vacant. It just doesn't have a minister for the moment.)

Aside from my regular duties and the additional ones as co-Interim moderator, I had been preparing an online course on the Apostles' Creed for elders of the Presbyterian Church in Canada. To make my work do double duty, I also preached through the creed in that vacant church. The extra work was not always easy, and my friends and family sometimes worried that I had taken too much on my plate. My colleague Bob and I often carried out our necessary church business by e-mail. One week I sent him an e-mail about some item of business. I added a quick p.s. about my planned sermon for the coming Sunday: "I'm descending into hell this week." I wrote, tongue in cheek. Almost immediately, I received a reply from my kindly colleague.

"I'm worried about you and how busy you are. Would you like me to preach for you this Sunday? Hell is a bad place to be."

Hell was just the subject of my sermon that week, but for many it's much more than that. It is a present and painful reality for many, even in the church. And Bob is right: hell is indeed a bad place to be. And hell sometimes breaks loose in church.

Why New People Come to Church

It's not all hell in the church, of course.

Early in my ministry a friend was involved in organizing a workshop on church growth led by the Crystal Cathedral Hour of Power *ministry, the Robert Schuller people. That was fine, except for the awkward fact that my friend also invited me and I didn't want to go. All that possibility-thinking stuff—I didn't want any of that, so I turned him down. But he kept asking and I kept saying "No, definitely not." Well, I kept saying no until, just as in the parable of the Widow and the Unjust Judge, it was less trouble to say yes than to keep on refusing. You will understand, then, that I showed up at the workshop with the worst possible attitude. I positively wanted the event to be terrible so I could enjoy the dubious pleasure of complaining about it.*

To my intense surprise, the workshop was terrific—full of good advice and intelligent strategies for looking at the church and the surrounding community through mission-shaped lenses. I chiefly remember a set of statistics provided about reasons new people show up in church. I no longer have the materials from the workshop, but I believe my memory is substantially correct. New attenders in churches of varied traditions in forty American states and seven Canadian provinces had been asked why they had decided to come to their new church. The answers were fascinating, and though the papers from the conference have disappeared in one of many moves, I think I remember the figures after all these years.

Because of mass evangelism	*.3% (Three out of a thousand!—negligible)*
Congregational outreach programs	*3–5%*
They liked the minister	*10–12%*
Because someone asked them	*85%*

Someone leaned over the back fence and said, "I'm finding help for my life in my church. Would you like to come with me next Sunday?" ("May I take you?" is much more effective than "Why don't you come?" at least in my experience.) The greatest evangelist in North America is not Billy Graham or any of his successors; it's the person who will lean over the back fence and invite the neighbor to church.

When I returned to my own congregation, I preached a sermon about all this. I remember that I said,

"I'll never ask you to knock on doors. I'll never ask you to hand out tracts. And I'll certainly never ask you to stand on the street corner wearing a sandwich board proclaiming, 'Repent. The end is near!' But I will ask you to speak about the Christian faith to people with whom you have other important conversations."

One person, a man named Andy, took that sermon seriously and in the next six months brought three new families to church.

There is one catch to all this.

Not too long after that workshop, I became a professor of preaching and moved away from that church. The advantage of not being the minister of a local church and preaching to the same people every Sunday is that you get to use the same material, the same stories, and the same statistics more than once. I have seen more recent statistics, and the exact percentages vary, depending on exactly what is asked. But some version of "someone asked me" is always at the top of the list of reasons people try a new church. I still like using the statistics I first came to know, however.

I remember using the statistics in a church where I was guest preacher, and I also used the image of "leaning over the back fence." As I was shaking hands at the church door after the service, a young woman approached me and said: "Funny you should say that about the back fence."

"Oh, why's that?"

The young woman half turned and pointed to a much older woman, the organist, still seated on the organ bench, "Because that woman lives over my back fence and she invited me to this church. I went into our house and I told my husband, 'We're going to go to the Presbyterian church.' 'Why in God's name would we want to do that?' he replied. 'Because our neighbor goes to that church, and I would like to grow to be the kind of woman that she is.'"

There is only one thing to say to that: Wow!

If both our words and our lives are inviting, just maybe, they will come.

The Rollex

I remember walking through the wonderful central street market in Seoul, South Korea, where almost anything was on sale, most definitely including watches. One vendor cornered me with a display of an amazing variety of watches for sale. He offered me a special deal, only ten dollars for a Swiss watch. I suspected, however, that the watch might be fake. In the first place, ten dollars is a price so low for a fine Swiss watch as to be not just amazing but unbelievable. And the second thing was that the name on the face of the watch was "Rollex," with two l's. That was fair, perhaps, since a one-l Rolex might cost a thousand times as much. Still, I passed on the deal.

The truth is that I am no expert on why people do or do not come to church. But I am pretty sure that if they do come, they want the real thing, not a cheap imitation of Christianity. We can't offer them a Rollex.

A Church in Assisi

Some years ago Patty and I spent two springtime weeks in Tuscany, Italy, renting with old friends a flat in a farmhouse set amid vineyards. Every day we would drive out to visit the churches, museums, galleries, and ancient towns of the region. To my surprise, even in those two weeks, between my knowledge of French and the remnants of my Latin, I was able to read considerable written Italian of the kind that may be found on historical plaques or in guidebooks. I was even able on occasion to take in some spoken Italian. It ought to have been and in many ways actually was a glorious experience. It was marred for me, however, by the uncomfortable truth that I had entered a period of spiritual dryness. I do not want to overstate this. I am not talking about the dark night of the soul or a spiritual dryness of Sahara Desert proportions—just a prolonged drought. It was real enough, however, and serious enough that I found it hard to pray.

I think it was hard for me to pray because day after day I was seeing and felt obligated to admire, masterworks of art that represented things that I as a Protestant did not believe . I began to feel, for example, that if I were faced with even one more representation of the Assumption of the Virgin Mary, I would burst. And it didn't matter if the painting was by Michelangelo or some other master, enough was enough! It is always, I think, a mistake to concentrate on what we cannot believe rather than on what we do believe.

So matters continued until very near the end of our stay. That day we decided to drive to the neighboring province of Umbria to visit Assisi, the home of Saint Francis, a figure whom I did admire. After driving for two hours, I remember well crossing a fertile valley and catching sight of Assisi, almost glowing a delicate pink in the morning sun, there on a mountainside above the farms in the wide valley below. The guidebook insisted that visitors who were interested in Francis—and most visitors to Assisi are—should most certainly make an extended stop at the church of Saint Mary of the Angels, on the flat land at the foot of the mountainside where the old city of Assisi was located. The guidebook was confusing, however. On the one hand, it seemed to speak of a chapel in which Francis and his brothers had prayed, and the cell where the saint had endured his final illness. On the other hand, the book described a church commenced in 1569 with money supplied by King Philip II of Spain. This church, the book claimed, was the seventh-largest church in Christendom. The description seemed to make no sense.

It was easy to find the church as we drove into town, for it was as large as the guidebook had promised. But it was rather ugly, in my view, far too large and ornate for the simple and austere life of Francis, and built in an architectural style I have never been able to admire. That, however, was not the most troubling side of the matter. The most troubling matter was the business of money for construction given by the king of Spain in 1569. I guessed, with some confidence, that the wealth behind the gift was wrung from the suffering peoples of Mexico, Peru, and the other Spanish colonies of the New World. That was surely one of the most shameful episodes in the long history of the church. This statement does not merely impose contemporary judgments upon a church of another time. Another admirable figure, Brother Bartolome de las Casas, excoriated in his day the cruelty of Spanish policies towards the indigenous people of the New World in A Short Account of the Destruction of the Indies.[1] I could not have had a more negative attitude as I entered the church.

At least I was negative until at the crossing of nave and transepts, dwarfed by the scale of the later church, I saw the Porziuncola, the tiny and roughly built ninth-century chapel where Francis had prayed. On the side was the rough cell where Francis had dwelled in his last years. As his death approached, he asked his brothers to lay him on the bare earth beside the cell so that he could die in utter poverty, in full solidarity with his Master, who had, as he himself said, no place to lay his head. I took my seat in the nave and listened as a Franciscan read aloud a Scripture lesson for the day, in

1. Las Casas, *Short Account of the Destruction of the Indies*.

Italian, as one might expect. Through the church his voice rang on the ears of visitors from around the world—some pilgrims, some, like me, tourists ticking off an entry in a guidebook. In a moment of Pentecost-like clarity, I could suddenly understand what I was hearing. "Silver and gold, have I none, but what I have I give you."[2] What a reading for Saint Francis! . . . And for me.

It was possible to enter the Porziuncola for a few moments. When it was my turn, I took my place near the rear of its simple nave at one of the unadorned kneelers. And I could pray.

I think I came very near that day to what might be called a stereotypically Protestant error, or perhaps more accurately, a Protestant oversimplification. I came very near to holding in utter contrast the outer and the inner churches—the proud and sinful church as an institution, on the one hand, and the simple, pure gospel within, the gospel of Francis himself. But I looked around me at the rough and simple construction of this little chapel, which represented that gospel in my eyes. I realized that had it been left to the elements, it would likely have fallen apart many centuries ago. Rather, it had been preserved by that grandiose surrounding structure that I had been so ready to hold in scorn.

The gospel does not exist on its own. It does not float, disembodied between heaven and earth. It is sheltered within the church, with all its many faults. Now, the history is still shameful. We can and must do better to purify the church so it can be a more fitting means for God's good ends. But it remains a place where the gospel, often when we least expect it, may be found.

It is recorded that Francis beheld the risen Christ in his initial vision and that one said to him, "Francis, Francis, go and repair My House which, as you can see, is falling into ruins." Perhaps, in our time, that is part of our task also.

2. The Scripture quotation is, more or less, from the King James Version, which was the version still used in my childhood and was impressed on my heart and mind in those formative years.

8

Stories of Grace

One hopes, not always successfully, that at the heart of the life of any Christian community is the experience of grace. Here are two stories I have included in earlier books. To my mind, both have something to do with grace.

Carlos

This is a story I used in a sample sermon in my book *Preaching That Matters*.[1] The sermon, titled "You Know!," was based on 2 Cor 8:9: "For you know the grace of our Lord Jesus Christ, that though he was rich, yet for your sake he became poor, so that you through his poverty might become rich."[2] In that part of 2 Corinthians, Paul is engaged in a very recognizable endeavor. He is trying to motivate the Corinthians to give, and to give generously. He uses various techniques we could easily recognize, including a reference to the generosity of the Macedonians, who give despite their own poverty. In the end, however, the chief motivation lies in something the Corinthians already know: the grace of the Lord Jesus. I tried to pick up both emphases in the following story. It comes from a visit I made to Brazil in 1991, a time of rampant poverty and hyperinflation.

---

1. Farris, *Preaching That Matters*, 145–46.

2. The quotation is from the NIV. The NRSV translation obscures Paul's repeated use of the word *grace* in this section of 2 Corinthians.

In Sao Paulo and in every Latin American city grow up on every open space what are called favelas, shack cities made of cardboard or tarpaper or plywood, or whatever the squatters can find. It would be dangerous for a person like me to go to a favela. Robbing me would be worth several months' income to anybody from a favela. But I and several others were taken to one favela by a man named Carlos, and with Carlos we were quite safe.

Carlos wasn't poor himself; he worked in a wire factory and earned a comfortable living. But some years earlier he had become troubled by the fact that the children of the favela near his apartment were not hearing the stories of Jesus. So one afternoon he walked over to the favela, sat down in an open space near the creek that flows like a fetid open sewer through the favela, and began to tell stories. And the children listened.

Then the adults started listening too. And if the adults are listening, you can't just tell Bible stories for children.

So he started a church service.

But if they're hungry, you can't just hold church services.

So he began to feed the children.

But it's much better if people help themselves rather than have others do all the work for them.

So he and his wife, Maria Josée, organized some of the women of the community to do the cooking. But you can't fill the belly and leave the mind empty.

So they began classes for the children to help them with school. But you can't just teach the children if the adults are ignorant.

So they began literacy classes for the adults.

But you can't just teach people to read if they can't get a job, and in that community being able to speak some English can help you get a job.

So they began English classes.

While I was there, the people of the little church were building an upper room—not for a pastor's study or a ladies' parlor or anything like that:

They were putting in a dentist's chair so that the inhabitants of the favela could have some dental care!

Well, the church folk gave us cornbread and thick, strong coffee and made us very welcome, but eventually it was time for us to return to our comfortable Western hotel.

I sat beside Carlos in his car, with an interpreter in the backseat. Carlos pulled out a photo of his family singing in church. There were Carlos and Maria Josée, whom we had met, and their three sons, of whom he had spoken so proudly.

And there, standing in the middle of the family, was a lovely, teenage girl. I said through the interpreter, "Who is the young lady?"

For the first time the smile left Carlos's face, and he replied, "That was our daughter; she died. She wanted to be a missionary, but she died of liver disease."

What do you say when you hear a story like that? I never know what to say, so I replied, again through the interpreter, "That must have been a terrible tragedy for you and Maria Josée."

And for his reply I needed no interpretation. "Yes" he replied, "but we are comforted. She is with Jesus."

There's something about the gospel.

There's something about the gospel that sends a man out, not once or twice, but again and again and again, into what is the worst hellhole I've ever seen on this planet.

There's something about the gospel that gives comfort and strength to a man and his wife when what to me as a parent is the worst of all human tragedies, the death of a child, happens.

There's something about the gospel.

One of the great gifts of traveling for the church to the poorer parts of the planet is that you meet some wonderful people. It makes you humble; they are so much better Christians than we are. I know that if in the kingdom of heaven I am within far shouting distance of Carlos and Maria Josée, I will be blessed indeed.

But of this I'm proud: The same gospel that gives strength and comfort to Carlos and Maria Josée is preached in our churches . . . and you know it already!

There's something about the gospel.

So when the day comes, and it will, when you ask, "Why give? Why work? Why bother?" you already know the answer.

"For you know the grace of our Lord Jesus Christ, that though he was rich, yet for your sake he became poor, so that you through his poverty might become rich."

You know!

As a Little Child

"Let the little children come to me; do not stop them; for it is to such as these that the kingdom of God belongs. Truly I tell you, whoever does not receive the kingdom of God as a little child will never enter it"(Mark 10:14b–15).

Some of my seminary classmates may recall the story differently, but this is the way I remember it happening.[3]

We were sitting in New Testament class under Professor Balmer Kelly when this passage came up for discussion. Professor Kelly turned to us and said, "Why like a little child?"[4]

One student raised a hand and asserted with considerable confidence, "Because little children are so naturally good and innocent."

Professor Kelly simply replied, "You don't have any children yet, do you?" It was true; that particular student had no children, and any parent could have refuted the notion of children's innocence from repeated experience.

Somebody else ventured another answer, "Because children are all humble."

Professor Kelly stroked his beard and asked, "Have you ever stood outside a schoolyard during recess and listened to the children?"

We all thought back to our grade school days: "I'm the king of the castle and you're the dirty rascal!" That answer was, by common accord, dismissed without a further thought. Several more possibilities were raised, each more unlikely than the last. Finally Professor Kelly looked at us with suitable professorial disgust. He reached into his pocket, pulled out his wallet and extracted a twenty-dollar bill. He walked over to a student named Don, the toughest, most hard-nosed man in the class, and gave the bill to him. Don turned approximately the shade of a Canadian Mountie's dress uniform.

---

3. This is a somewhat expanded version of a story I used to begin and to close Farris, *Grace*.

4. Nowadays a student might advance a suitably contemporary political interpretation that children are marginalized and have no power. I doubt if Professor Kelly would have been impressed. Children were valued in the world of Israel's Scriptures. "Blessed are those whose quiver is full of them!" Though a child might have no power, if he (the gender specific pronoun is intended) was the son of a wealthy family, he would inherit wealth and power in due course. That is the point of Paul's comparison of the law to the *paidogogos*—to the slave who temporarily bore authority over the heir. If Mark's Jesus had intended to say that his followers must identify with the marginalized and oppressed, there would have been far easier and clearer ways to say so.

"You don't like me giving you money, do you?" said Professor Kelly. "You're going to try to give it back to me after the class, but I'm not going to take it." That Don didn't like it was manifest; he was holding the bill by its absolute tip as if it were covered with a particularly nasty acid that was burning the tips of his fingers.

"Now if I asked you to come over to my house to do some yard work or to help me move some books and I paid you for your work, you wouldn't mind at all." There were nods of agreement all around.

"But what if I gave the money to a child?"

No further words were necessary for the picture of a child reaching out a hand to receive what had not been earned, a child who thought it the most natural thing in the world to receive a gift, that picture was there before us.

Whoever does not receive the kingdom of God as a little child . . .

I think that I remember this story so clearly because I had been struggling with exactly that issue then. I had attended the University of Toronto, lived at home, and commuted to school. With some scholarship money, long hours working during holidays, and the fact that tuition was so much lower in those distant days, I had managed to pay tuition and all other direct costs myself. I took pride in that. But then the call to ministry came unmistakably to me, and after initial resistance, I gave in. Because of my family circumstances as the son of a theology professor well known in Canadian Presbyterian circles, it seemed best to enroll in a theological school in the United States. There, I hoped, I would not be known primarily as my father's son. Besides, Dad really did not want to have to teach me. This was a problem, however. The tuition was so much higher in the U.S., and then there would be the cost of travel, and room and board on top of tuition. There was no possible way that I could meet the costs. They was simply beyond me.

My parents called me, and I recall what I think were their exact words: "Stephen, we think you were made to be a minister. You're our son and we love you. We want to help you financially."

I took the money. Looking back on all that, I think this is the real question: When did I become mature in my relationship with my parents? Was it when I paid my own way? Now, that was important and valuable; it is certainly not a good thing for children to sponge off their parents. Or was it when I stretched out my hand to receive, because I was their child and they loved me?

Whoever does not receive the kingdom of God as a little child . . .

What Happens with the Money

Still, it was not easy to receive, even from parents and, perhaps as a reminder to myself, I have used the story of Professor Kelly and the twenty-dollar bill many times over the years, with many different groups. When I do so, I always give away a bill, though sometimes not a twenty, and only occasionally has the recipient tried to give the money back to me later. I always figure that anybody who tries to do that has missed the point. But usually they get it—both the money and the point.

Occasionally, I hear later what happened to the money. Some years ago I was to speak on grace in a Methodist church in Texas. I decided to begin the series with the story about Professor Kelly and the twenty-dollar bill. When I tell this story, I always give the money to a man, if possible. This is not sexism, I think. It is because in my experience men have more trouble receiving than do women. The main other criterion for choosing a victim is that I can get to him easily from the pulpit. If possible, however, I also choose a man who looks grumpy. That is not always so easy, but on this occasion I looked out and to my right was a perfect candidate, a man, sitting at the end of a pew near the front of the church, and, my oh my, he looked grumpy. He was a big man, arms folded across the belly, mouth pulled down in a serious frown. In fact, he looked like the stereotypical movie version of a southern sheriff. Put one of those Smokey the Bear police hats on him, strap a six shooter to his waist, and place a radar gun in his hand, and he would look as if he had come directly from central casting. I found out later that I had spectacularly misread the man. He was in fact one of the sweetest-tempered people in the church—we should never judge from appearances—but at the moment he looked like a perfect candidate. Despite his appearance, he received the money graciously. (It's interesting how well that word fits!)

Sometime later, the minister of the church wrote me to tell me what the man had done with the money. On the hottest day of a Texas summer, he used that money and doubtless some of his own to take the children of the church out for ice cream after the service and told them that Jesus loved them. What a lovely and creative thing to do with what he had been given!

On another occasion, a man in Toronto who had received the bill let me know that he had a friend who taught art in a school in a slum area in Kingston, Jamaica. If anyone has only stayed in an all-inclusive resort in Jamaica, they have not visited the real Jamaica. It is, in places, a dreadfully poor country. Whether in a rich or a poor country, however, we all know what goes first when cuts have to be made in educational spending. It is almost always spending on music and the arts. It's hard to imagine how little that teacher would have in the way of resources for her class. The man in Toronto took the money I had given him and doubtless some of his own and sent it to his friend to buy art supplies for her class. Once, again what a beautiful and creative thing to do!

So, do we simply receive, sit back, do nothing, and that's it for the Christian life? Not at all!

Perhaps this is the nature of Christian life: to receive what God gives in Christ and then to figure out something lovely and creative to do with what we have first been given.

A Coda

On one occasion, I was teaching a class of candidates for the office of permanent deacon in the Roman Catholic Archdiocese of Toronto. Normally, in the Roman Catholic Church, the diaconate is a way station on the road to the priesthood. But recently the authorities in a number of dioceses, perhaps motivated the shortage of priestly vocations, have recruited married men to be educated as deacons and to remain in that office for life. These permanent deacons are then able to relieve the priests of a considerable number of their duties. Because this is a relatively new program and the candidates are therefore very carefully screened, the group is always made up of high-quality people. I thoroughly enjoy teaching them. As I expected, the chosen "victim" received the bill, this time a ten, with "good grace."

The day after the program ended, I went down to my office. The program takes place out of the academic terms, and my trip was unplanned. To my surprise, I saw one of the permanent deacon candidates, in fact, the one to whom I had given the money, bending down and slipping an envelope under my office door. He looked very embarrassed when he saw me. I greeted him politely, of course. He flushed, handed me the envelope, mumbled something about wanting to thank me for my part in the program, and bolted out the door. I assumed there was a thank-you card in the envelope, thought, how kind! and began the administrivial duties that had taken me down to my office.

When I had finished my tasks, I finally got around to opening the envelope. There was no card but inside was a folded piece of notepaper. On the outside was written, "Mark 4:20. 'And these are the ones sown on the good soil: they hear the word and accept it and bear fruit, thirty and sixty and a hundredfold.'"

Inside the notepaper was a thousand-dollar bill.

Amazing! But then, there is always something amazing about grace.

9

The Sacraments

BAPTISM

A Baptism in Debrecen

One of the richest experiences of my life was to serve a term as a member of the Executive Committee of the then World Alliance of Reformed Churches (WARC). WARC was the umbrella organization of Presbyterian and Reformed Churches around the world. (It is now called the World Communion of Reformed Churches or WCRC.) My term culminated with the 1997 General Council of that organization, held in the ancient Reformed city of Debrecen, Hungary. Debrecen is a city that stayed Protestant through the rule of the Turks, the persecuting ultra-Catholic dynasty of the Hapsburgs, the Nazis, and the Communists. The famous old Reformed high school in Debrecen was reputed to be the only Christian school east of the Iron Curtain that never closed under the Communists.

In a world conference, a very large percentage of participants can speak English either as a native tongue or a second, third or fourth language. When it was announced that for the first Sunday of the conference the sermon would be translated into English at the "Little Church" of Debrecen, most participants, whatever their national origin, decided to attend. The "Little Church" seats about 1,200 people, and by the time my wife and I arrived, it was nearly full . In honor of the event, many wore their national costumes. It was quite a sight!

The service began with a celebration of the sacrament of baptism. A very young couple, perhaps in their teens, holding what was very likely their first precious child, was led to the font. The young mother looked around; saw an enormous congregation drawn from every race and most nationalities around the world, standing to recognize and to welcome her child. She burst into tears.

We are not baptized into our local congregations only. We are all baptized into the body of Christ, the holy catholic church, a great and noble fellowship . What is true of every baptism was simply more visibly true that day.

What Allan Says about Baptism

My son Allan is now a minister, and he has told me what he says when he is visiting parents who have requested baptism for a child. He says he tells them that baptism is like giving up your child for adoption. It is recognizing that somebody else can be a better father, a better parent than you can. And then you receive the child back from that parent to nurture. I doubt that Allan could think of baptism that way if he had not handed over his own two children in exactly that way.

I was the one who was privileged to baptize them into the one, holy, catholic, and apostolic church. Good moments!

Some Other Debrecen Stories

These two anecdotes may not strictly belong here in a collection of stories about the sacraments. They come from my time in Debrecen, however, and it may be convenient to include them here.

Outside Pressure

When I was in Hungary, the Reformed Church was feeling great pressure from American organizations sending missionaries to the newly accessible countries of Eastern Europe to establish churches that often drew away worshipers from Reformed congregations that were already struggling from years of Communist oppression. One Hungarian minister drew me aside and told me, "We survived the Turks. We survived the Hapsburgs, the Nazis, and the Communists. We may not survive the American evangelicals." This is not to say that no missionaries from the West should go to the former East bloc. Rather, it is to say that those missionaries ought to work cooperatively and respectfully with the Christian churches there who remained faithful through the hard times.

The second matter requires some historical background but must be told in justice to the Roman Catholic Church and, specifically, to Pope John Paul II. This story was also told to me by a minister from Debrecen. Many stories will come to us if we show ourselves ready to listen.

The Pope in Debrecen

The reason a church that seats 1,200 people is called the little church is that another Reformed Church in the city seats more than three thousand: the Nagy Templom, or Great Church of Debrecen. Immediately behind the Great Church is a monument to the Galley Slaves of Debrecen. These were Reformed ministers of Debrecen who refused to recant their Protestant faith during a bitter persecution in the time of the ultra-Catholic Hapsburg dynasty. In 1673 more than forty ministers of the Debrecen region were sentenced to serve as slaves in the galleys of the king of Naples. According to the storyteller, churches in the Protestant lands of western and northern Europe tried to ransom the slaves, without effect. Doubtless the king of Naples did not wish to offend the powerful Hapsburgs by freeing the galley slaves.

This sad state of affairs lasted until February 11, 1676, when a Dutch admiral named Michael de Ruyter led his naval squadron into the harbor of Naples and, in the words of my informant, "reasoned with" the authorities. It takes little imagination to guess the nature of the reasoning. The authorities saw reason, and the twenty six surviving ministers were freed and handed over to the Dutch. They were given safe haven in Protestant churches (most notably in Zurich), received medical treatment and other support until they had regained their strength, and eventually returned to their homeland. It happened that among the participants in the general council of the Alliance of Reformed Churches was a descendant of one of the ministers and also a descendant of Admiral de Ruyter. A photo of the two descendants was taken, under the shadow of the monument.

It is right and proper to honor the memory of those who, in the words of the monument's inscription, were deported "for faith and gospel freedom."[1] They are the spiritual ancestors of present-day Reformed Christians like me. It is also right to remember all those who have suffered for conscience, most of whom have no monument other than our freedom. And, on an occasion such as a General Council of a world communion, it is also right to celebrate an example of solidarity in the support of those undergoing persecution. But the matter cannot be left there. To remember only stories such as this one can allow a person like me to think of myself as heir only of the victims of persecution.

The sad truth is that just about any tradition that has ever exercised power also has episodes in its history we would rather not remember. It happens, for example, that I am writing this chapter while sitting in a house in a village in the south of France. It was historically a Catholic village that grew up around an abbey founded during the reign of Charlemagne in the late eighth century. Very little remains of the ancient or medieval village, however. The abbey and the surrounding village were destroyed in 1562 during the French Wars of Religion, by Huguenots, French Protestants, also my spiritual ancestors. Most of us are also heirs of persecutors or at least, perpetrators of violence.

Thankfully, the story is not quite complete. My Hungarian friend went on to tell me that Pope John Paul II visited Debrecen in 1991 and spoke in the Great Church. "I am well aware that this meeting would not have been possible in former times. A pope visiting Hungary would not have come to Debrecen. The citizens of Debrecen would not have desired his presence."[2]

The pope was informed of the nature of the monument to the galley slaves. He took the time in a busy papal schedule to visit the monument and to pray, in sorrow for the past and with hope for reconciliation in the present and in the future. He laid a wreath at the foot of the monument. There is

1. The Latin inscription as a whole might be translated as, "A monument to the ministers of the divine word who, for faith and gospel freedom, were deported from Hungary to the Neapolitan triremes." A *trireme* is a galley with three banks of oars. Photos of the monument and of the inscription may be found here: http://www.allaboutshipping.co.uk/2015/09/27/a-dutch-admiral-who-rescued-from-the-galleys-men-persecuted-for-their-faith/. Or they may be found here: http://wikimapia.org/25674908/hu/Gályarabok-emlékoszlopa/. (Click to enlarge the thumbnail.)

2. The text of the pope's address may be found here: https://w2.vatican.va/content/john-paul-ii/en/speeches/1991/august/documents/hf_jp-ii_spe_19910818_celebraz-ecum-debrecen.html/.

now yet one more monument in Debrecen, a bronze replica of the wreath the pope left that day.[3]

You might consider this second monument a sign that there is always hope for reconciliation. And, perhaps, if our hearts begin to heal from historical hatreds, with the help of the Holy Spirit, even a monument can be an outward and visible sign of an inward and invisible grace. Perhaps this story has something to do with sacraments after all.

COMMUNION

Aunt Letty

When I was a boy our family shared all the special events—Christmas, Thanksgiving, and so on—with the family of my Aunt Letty. I remember when I was very young, barely able to see over a table, I wandered into the kitchen. There on the kitchen table, at the level of my eyes, was the great golden bird, steaming hot with rich aromas promising wonders yet to come. Aunt Letty caught sight of my staring eyes. With a knife, she nipped off a tidbit, just a tidbit, and offered it to me.

She said, "This is because you're special and I love you."

Communion says, "You are special and God loves you." The bread and wine of the Lord's Supper are a tidbit, just a tidbit, that points back to the sacrifice of Christ for us. It makes present in our midst the reality of a past event. How this happens I will not attempt to specify here. That it happens, in the present, is enough for me. But according to an ancient teaching of the church, the sacrament also points forward—forward to the feast of the kingdom of God to come. That truth might seem a little dry and scholastic, if it were not for that story and the next.

3. A photo of the replica of the wreath may be found here: http://www.allabout-shipping.co.uk/2015/09/27/a-dutch-admiral-who-rescued-from-the-galleys-men-persecuted-for-their-faith/. Or it may be found here: http://wikimapia.org/25674908/hu/Gályarabok-emlékoszlopa/. (Click to enlarge the thumbnail.)

Operation Manna

Early in my teaching career I had a student named Laurent, who was con-
siderably older than I was. One day after class Laurent, who had been raised
in the Netherlands, spoke to me about the terrible winter of 1944-45 in his
homeland. The Allied armies had been held up in the waterlogged southern
part of the country and by a strategic concentration on thrusting forward
into the heart of Germany itself. In the meantime, the people of the most
heavily populated parts of the country remained under occupation and the
population was in a dreadful condition.

Many thousands starved to death that terrible winter, and more were
on the verge of death by starvation. This came to the attention of the Allied
Chiefs in London, and through the mediation of the Swedish Red Cross a
partial truce was arranged. That organization managed to ship flour into
the country. More surprisingly, the Germans agreed to allow Allied bombers
laden with food supplies to fly in low and slow over the countryside, dropping
foodstuffs by parachute. The bombers came in at three thousand feet, point
blank range for antiaircraft artillery, but the Germans honored the agree-
ment and held their fire.

Laurent said he could still remember vividly the first meal made with
those supplies, that manna from the heavens. He particularly remembered
the bread; it was sweet, he said, and wonderful to the taste. But, he said,
it more than met their present need. It was also a promise of what was to
come. The long night of occupation and oppression would end, and freedom
would come at last. The bread was a promise of what was yet to come. But
come it surely would.

So it is with the bread and wine of communion. It reminds us of what
God has done in Christ for us. It makes present to us in this moment
his sacrifice for us. It is a promise of what is yet to come. And come it
surely shall. Give us, we pray, that bread, the bread that meets our needs
today and the bread that holds within itself the promise of your future
kingdom.

The Little Church in Debrecen

But now I must turn back to that Sunday in Debrecen: A choir from across
the border in the Ukraine was there to sing that day and took its place in
the balcony very close to where I was seated. The choir director was an older

woman, quite fierce looking, as if determined that everything should go well on this day of days. If any choir members dared whisper or giggle, she glared at them as if daring them to be anything but remain solemn.

The preacher was an older minister, also from the Ukraine. I was told after the service that, as a young minister, he had been arrested by the KGB in 1946 for corrupting youth . . . by preparing them for confirmation. The KGB had sneaked a camera into the church and had photographed him confirming these young people.

He was arrested, confronted with the photos and asked, "Who is doing this?" Life was all ahead of him (he had recently become engaged), but he did not deny his role. "Who else would it be?" he replied. He was sentenced to ten years' hard labour in a Siberian prison camp, the gulag. Did his Christian faith seem foolish those long years in the gulag? Was there any point in standing up against these forces?

In 1953 the dictator Stalin died, and many political prisoners were released as part of an amnesty. Among the released prisoners was the no-longer young minister who made his way home to the Ukraine. His fiancée had waited for him. She was the choir director that morning in Debrecen. No wonder she wanted things to go right!

When the choir sang, they sang in Hungarian an old gospel hymn based on the story of Jesus walking on the water. In the hymn the disciples complain to the master, "Do you not care, Master?" And Jesus responds, "Peace. Be still. Do you not know that even the winds and the waves obey me?" And the Hungarians, who could understand the words and had lived through the long night of oppression, wept.

It is into this fellowship that you have been baptized, and it is with these sisters and brothers that you share the Lord's Supper.

Open our eyes, Lord, so that we may see what is true.

Bread Laid Out for Us

A number of years ago I attended a meeting hosted by a large church in central Sao Paulo, Brazil. Sao Paulo is an enormous city of twenty-nine million people by some estimates, with great shack cities called favelas, homes to millions of the appallingly poor, but poverty is by no means confined to the favelas. One day I noticed a man lying in the open gallery covering the sidewalk outside the church door. His clothes were torn and stained; to all appearances he was sleeping it off. There was nothing unusual in this. The like could be seen in any large city here in Canada also. But this was different: by his head, laid in preparation for the hour when he should awake, there was a handkerchief, white as the linen on the Holy Table. And on that cloth were five small loaves. I asked about what I had seen and was told that he had been an educated man from a wealthy family, fluent in three foreign languages, but he had drunk away his life with a bottle. From time to time, if sober, he would do a little outside work at the church, but he refused steadfastly ever to enter the church itself. It was as if he felt unworthy to come into the house of God.

I suppose it was foolish to lay out the loaves for the man. There were poor by the millions in that city, and what were five small loaves compared to that mass of misery? And were not many of those other poor millions more deserving than this man who had wasted his life on a bottle? So a realist might think. To lay a table for this man might seem truly foolish—as foolish, perhaps as trying to feed five thousand with a small boy's lunch.

I was called on to express our thanks to our hosts at the conclusion of the meetings. I spoke of what I had seen—mentioning in particular the man sleeping outside the church door—and of how touched I was, how touched we all were, by the faith and courage of the church to venture what they had even in the face of overwhelming poverty. I think our hosts were touched in their turn by what I said.

The next year that same committee met in another country. The minister of the Sao Paulo church, who was also a member of the committee, approached me.

"Do you remember the man you spoke of last year?"

"Yes," I replied.

"He died," said the minister. "But before that, he allowed us to carry him inside, and he died surrounded by friends, in the church."

In a realist's world, offering bread to this man did not amount to much. Surely, it was not the feeding of five thousand. In truth, it was not much at all. But in Jesus's world, this is what it was: a miracle, a sign of the glory and the power of Jesus. And sometimes, sometimes when my small supply of faith is strong, Jesus's world seems more powerful and more real than any world the realist may know.

I offer a note about this story: it happens that this is my only story whose truthfulness has been directly challenged by a listener. "Oh, come on!" he said. "That isn't true."

It also happens that this is the only story of which I have photographic proof. I have a picture on my desk of the man and the five small loaves.

10

Bicycle Stories

These are three stories that all began life the same way, as children's stories. Many so-called children's stories are not so much stories as object lessons: "Guess what I have in the paper bag, children." I myself am sometimes tempted to think that the most accurate answer to this leading question for many a children's sermon would be, something you found in the backseat of your car on the way to church. But that may be ungenerous. Some people have the gift of telling object lesson children's stories very effectively. It may be, however, that the ability to imagine a link between the object in the lesson and whatever spiritual reality we want to convey may not yet be developed in younger children around us. That is probably true also about the stories in this chapter. But children do have an uncanny ability to listen to stories on a wide variety of levels.

Painted Pink

I learned to ride a bicycle the year my baby sister, Marion, was born. I was eight years old at the time and very tall for my age. All the other kids on the block were on two-wheelers, even ones that were much smaller and obviously just little kids, but I was stuck with a tricycle. So I asked my parents for a bicycle. There wasn't much money in the family that year, what with a new baby sister arriving, and all that my father could scrounge up was five dollars. Even long, long ago when I was eight years old, five dollars was not enough to buy very much of a bike but Dad did manage to find one for that price. It had a frame, handlebars, pedals, and chain—but that was it. There was nothing more, no fenders, no handgrips, no bell, no chain guard and, most important, no seat. There was that tube thing that sticks up at the back that the seat is attached to (I believe that the technical term is the seat *post). But there was no seat.*

So Dad went down into the basement, found a piece of three-quarter-inch plywood and with a coping saw (one of those saws that can cut curves), cut the wood into the shape of a bicycle seat. He attached the handcrafted seat to the seatpost, rounded the edges with a rasp and sandpapered it until it was smooth and, thank heavens, sliver free. He stepped back, considered his handiwork and said to me, "You know, a bicycle is going to be outside in the rain and snow. That's not good for untreated wood. We need to find some paint, or varnish or shellac to protect the seat."

The only trouble was that there was neither shellac nor varnish in the house, and the only paint was from the can left over from painting my new baby sister's bedroom. It was, as you might guess, a very pleasant shade of baby-sister pink. But I was eager to ride my very own bicycle so I certainly was in no mood to object. So the seat was painted pink.

"When can I learn to ride my bike?" I asked excitedly.

"Not for a while yet, son. It will take at least three hours for the paint to dry."

But patience is rarely a strongly developed virtue among eight-year-old boys, and after barely an hour I slipped in the basement and tested the paint. To my disappointment, it was still wet. Not too long later I tried again—still wet. Every few minutes I would test the paint until, after about two hours had elapsed, I tested the paint and . . . dry!

"Dad, come down and check the paint now. It's dry!" So Dad made his way down the stairs, felt the seat gingerly with one finger, then laid his entire hand on it.

"It is dry! That's surprising. It shouldn't be ready for an hour yet–old paint, I guess."

Together we pushed the bike out onto the street in front of our house. Dad held the bike while I balanced on the pink-painted seat and stretched my feet down to the pedals for the first time. He gave me a good push in the back, ran with me, held me and picked me up when, as happened many times, I fell.

He ran with me and held me, and picked me up when I fell. Over and over again, he ran with me and held me, and picked me up when I fell, until at last I could ride a bicycle on my own. At last I was satisfied. I dismounted for the last time, and Dad got a good look at me. It turned out that the paint wasn't dry after all. There on the seat of my blue jeans was a blotch of baby-sister pink paint. Between the shape of the bicycle seat and the contours of my rear end, the blotch looked for all the world like a badly drawn Valentine's heart crayoned by a kindergarten child who couldn't keep within the lines.

I didn't like the idea of having a pink valentine on my rear end, and I cannot even remember what my mother said when she saw my trousers. I doubt she was very happy! But when I think back to that heart, I'm happy. Because a valentine's heart is a symbol of love, and I know my parents loved me. That's why they spared five dollars to buy me a bike when money must have been terribly short. And, above all, that's why my Dad ran with me and held me, and picked me up when I fell.

I can ride a bicycle without any help now, and in case, my dad is long dead. But some falls in life hurt a good deal more than a tumble from a bicycle. No matter how old we get or how tall we grow, we still need somebody to run with us and hold us and pick us up when we fall.

And that, I think, is what Jesus does. If we let him, he will always run with us and hold us, and pick us up when we fall.

Here's a final note: When I tell this as a children's story, a potential problem arises. What about children who do not have a loving father? Or, more commonly, what about children whose father does not live with them for a wide variety of reasons? Then, of course, some children have fathers who are emotionally distant or abusive. Will I add to their hurt by telling a story about the kind of loving and present father that they do not have? Or the negative reaction might come from an adult rather than the children themselves (perhaps vicariously on behalf of the children), but I don't want to hurt adults either. Perhaps this is a story that should not be told in public, where the speaker has little or no knowledge of the family circumstances of children in the group. Perhaps it should be saved, for example, to tell to the grandchildren.

However, almost any story powerful enough to touch the heart, and certainly any story that speaks specifically about personal relationships, has the capacity to hurt some listener. If we avoid that kind of story, we will end up telling only tales with the emotional depth of TV shows about purple dinosaurs or saccharine sweet bears. Still, the problem is real. This story and others like it must therefore be told in a gentle and serious manner, and it is best to face the problem directly. When I'm telling this story in public, I say near the end, "I know that some children don't have dads, and that's sad. And some children do have dads, but their dads don't seem to love them as well as their children would like. That's very sad too."

The Wind

This is a story that my father told me when I was a boy. In turn, I told this story to my boys when they were little. But that wasn't the beginning of the story: my dad's grandfather, my great-grandfather, told it to my father when he was a boy. That makes this a very old family story indeed!

In the late nineteenth century when my great-grandfather was a young man, he bought for himself a bicycle with the new rubber tires that made bicycles so very much more practical and easy to ride. At that time he lived on the family farm near the shores of Lake Huron. Lake Huron is, to my mind, the most beautiful of all the Great Lakes, but sometimes the winds blow hard and cold off its wide expanse. But even if the winds were blowing so hard that a person could hardly stand, Scots Presbyterians like my great-grandfather kept the Sabbath by going to church on Sunday. The Sunday after he purchased his new bicycle, he decided to ride it to church.

But, he discovered, the wind was blowing off the lake and directly in his face as he pedaled to church. Now cyclists know how very difficult and slow a business it is to pedal even a bike with newly invented rubber tires against a strong wind. Great-grandfather puffed and sweated but made only very slow progress. In fact, he was late for church. He made his way shamefacedly to the only empty pew, in the very front of the church, of course. These were Presbyterians, after all. The elders with their black frock coats, their long beards, and longer faces stared at him with disapproval in their thoroughly Calvinist eyes. Great-grandfather was deeply embarrassed, and so when the time for prayers came, he begged God, "Please, dear God, please change the wind!" And, said my great-grandfather, "God must have decided to teach me a lesson. Because God did change the wind!"

And my great-grandfather pedaled all the way home . . . against the wind.

This is one of the stories about which people ask me, "Is that true?" By which they mean, of course, did it happen? And the answer is, I don't know. Quite possibly not. But that is the way my father told me the story.

More significantly, at least one of the lessons we could draw from the story is not true in the more important sense of the word. I do not think it is true that we need to watch very carefully what we pray for lest God play a cruel joke on us and give what we ask for. I do not think it is true that God is like that. But it is true, I think, that we don't always know what to ask for in our prayers and that "No" is sometimes the kindest answer to our prayers.

And the matter of answers to prayer leads to another story.

The Bicycle Chain

This is one of those cases where telling one story generates another. A man named Michael heard me tell the story about the pink bicycle seat, and after church he told me this story.

Michael told me his father was strict, so very strict that Michael was, in fact, a little bit afraid of his father. Now the word strict *does not mean "cruel" or "nasty." Strict means . . . Well, there may be a teacher in your school who is strict. When that teacher tells you to do something, you do it because you know there will be trouble if you do not! And you may be a little scared of that teacher too. Nevertheless, Michael decided to ask his father for a bicycle. His father said what many parents say: 'I'll think about it.'"*

A day or two later, Michael's father arrived home with a brand new bike. "Michael," he said, "This is a very expensive bicycle, and I am giving it to you because I think you are old enough and responsible enough to care for it properly. If you do not look after it, I will be very disappointed in you. Enjoy your new bicycle."

"Yes, Dad! Yes, Dad!" said Michael.

Michael happily cycled away and when he was a long ride from home, the chain fell off the sprockets and gears. If you ride a bicycle, you will know that this means that no matter how hard you pedal, you won't go anywhere. There was nothing Michael could do about this. So Michael pushed his bicycle slowly and sadly back towards his home.

And all the way home, he could hear his father's voice, "I am giving this bicycle to you because I think you are old enough and responsible enough to care for it properly."

Push, push, push.

"If you do not look after it, I will be very disappointed in you."

Push, push, push.

"I will be very disappointed in you."

Push, push, push.

When he arrived home, he pushed the bicycle into the garage and hid it behind some empty cardboard boxes so his father would not see the chain hanging limp and useless. That night in his bed Michael said his prayers.

After all, his parents, his Sunday school teacher, and his minister had told him that God answers our prayers and he decided to take their words seriously.

"Dear God," he prayed. "Please, please put the chain back on the bicycle!"

And he drifted off to sleep quite confident that God would answer his prayer. Early the next morning he awakened, slipped down to the garage and removed the cardboard boxes that had been concealing the bike. He eagerly looked to see the answer to his prayer, and . . . the chain was still off the bicycle.

Gathering up his courage, he approached his father and said with trepidation, "Dad, I tried my very best to look after my bike, but yesterday when I was riding it, the chain fell off my bike!" And he waited for his father to blast him.

"That's all right," said his father. "That happens all the time. I'll show you how to fix it."

And they went together into the garage and put the chain back on the bicycle.

At this point, if I am telling this as a children's story, I generally stop and ask the kids if Michael's prayer was answered. They usually look a bit puzzled and then one of them says, probably with uncertainty, "Yes."

I think so too. In fact, I think the prayer was answered in three separate ways. In the first place the prayer was answered on a quite literal level. The chain was, after all, back on the bicycle. Moreover, Michael had learned a skill every cyclist should possess: how to put a chain back on a bicycle. When I tell this story in church, I say that there is a trick to putting a chain back on a bicycle, and if they want to learn how to do it, come talk to me after church. Sometimes they do come and ask me, mostly because their fathers encourage them to do so, I think. (Turn the bicycle upside down so it rests on its seat and its handlebars. Fit the chain onto the nearest tooth in the front sprocket, Turn the pedal to draw the chain onto the rest of the sprocket. Easy peasy. Though bicycle gears seem to be so much better built now than in Michael's youth (or mine) that chains rarely seem to fall off these days.) But back to the story: most important, Michael had learned something about his father. His father was not as terrifyingly strict as he had thought. Not bad.

Anybody who seriously tries praying knows that you don't always get what you want, to parody an old Rolling Stones song. Prayer is not like Harry Potter–style magic. We cannot wave a wand, even one with a phoenix tail core, say "Oremus," and get whatever we want. It doesn't work that way, and it is not just that way with self-centered "shopping list" prayers. ("O Lord, won't you buy me a Mercedes Benz.") Sometimes, painfully often, we pray generously for the right things and the right people with hearts full of love, and what we ask for just doesn't happen. But I can say this, and people who know far more about prayer than I do will confirm this: If we pray, we do get to know the Father. We get to know God, and that is truly more wonderful than anything else we could possible ask for in our prayers.

11

Telling Stories Outside the Church

Sometimes we come upon opportunities to address the world beyond the walls of the church. This can be challenging, for many in that wider audience will have negative reactions to Christians in general and clergy in particular. Whether these negative feelings, sometimes amounting to fixed prejudices, are justified is not the issue. They will be present whether we like it or not and therefore must be taken into account. Many people, if they know they are being addressed by someone from the church, will say or think, "Don't preach at me!" Even a hint that a Christian author or speaker is claiming some kind of moral authority or is displaying spiritual condescension, whether real or imagined, will be fatal to effective communication. Telling a story may, however, work around those feelings, at least in some cases.

When I was a minister of a small congregation near Kingston, Ontario, I became known outside the church for two reasons. One was that I coached a local high school basketball team for two seasons. This was not particularly successful on the court; we were a middle-of-the-pack team. But it did mean that I had contacts with the youth of the area that could not have been gained in any other way. For the purposes of this book, however, the second reason is more significant. I entered the short story contest held by Canada's largest newspaper, the *Toronto Star*. No, I did not win, but in my third year of trying, my entry was awarded a "Judges' Choice" and was published. People did notice, and some of them took the time to talk with me about the issue behind the story.

In the early and middle 1980s the Canadian legal system did not take drunken driving seriously enough. In several well-publicized cases, drunken driving had cost the lives of innocent victims, but surprisingly lenient sentences had been imposed. The phrase "getting away with murder" appeared in some of the news stories about the trials. Moreover, I recalled that one of the stalwarts of my congregation had told me that she had lost her mother to a drunk driver. Her mother had been on her way home from a meeting of the Women's Christian Temperance Union. All that led to my entry for the 1985 contest. The story is dated since the legal system now takes drunken driving more seriously, particularly when it results in death or injury. I do not think for a minute that my story had any direct influence on that change. But perhaps it did contribute in a very small way to the general climate of opinion, shared not only by church folk but also other people of goodwill, which did, in the end, affect sentencing. As I read the story now, I have to admit that it would be the better for some editing, but here it is as it appeared in the newspaper. Perhaps it can illustrate in a small way what can be done with storytelling outside the church.

I Am a Murderer

"I am a murderer."

(Good start. That's got them.)

"Principal Wright, members of the teaching staff, students. I'm not exaggerating; I am a murderer."

(Pause, two, three, go)

"I say that because, to put it to you absolutely straight, I killed a man. In fact, I killed my business partner. I killed my best friend. And if you follow my path, you might do the same. You too might have to look into the mirror and say:

'I am a murderer.'"

(Good, let that sink in.)

"I'm here to talk to you about drinking and driving, of course. Now, I'm not going to preach to you; I'm not the prison chaplain; they let him go home at night!"

(Wait for the laughter to stop.)

"I'm not going to tell you to flee demon rum. I'm not going to tell you never to take a drink. But I am going to tell you what can happen if you drink and drive; I'm going to tell you my story. Most of you people are, what? Fourteen to eighteen, nineteen? Is that right, Principal?"

(Turn, wait for him to nod.)

"You guys especially must be wondering 'What is it that makes a man a man?'" Maybe you think it's booze. Well. I'm forty-two, and I was wondering too. You've heard of the midlife crisis? I was in it. Lots of guys my age are. Here I was, partner in a successful business, had what I'd been working for ever since university, and I was saying to myself, 'Is this all there is?' I began to buy myself toys. You know the difference between a man and a boy? It's the cost of his toys."

(That one missed. Wrong touch.)

"My toys were expensive. For instance, I bought myself one of those big four-wheel-drive pickups. Real macho, eh? Anything to tell myself I was a man. I also picked up a place on the lake, west of the city, to impress the ladies, you know. And I used to love chugging along out to my place in my four-by-four. Kind of silly, perhaps, but harmless.

"Until I started chugging something else, that is. You've heard of the three-martini lunch? Well, I hate martinis, but you get the idea. And every day as business began to slow down, I began to tie one on. Bourbon usually; the good ol' boys drink bourbon in the movies, right? My secretary knew what was going on; she pretended not to notice. One day Jim, my partner, drove home behind me; he had a place in the west end too, in Bay View up on the hill across the tracks.

"Man," he said, "You were weaving all over the place last night. I was almost scared driving along behind you. Why don't you cut back a bit on the sauce?"

"Fine," I told him. "You drive ahead of me and you won't have to worry!"

"Won't have to worry!"

(Pause; shake the head; look penitent. Go.)

"So, after that I always waited for Jim to leave first. I didn't mind; it gave me time for one more for the road. For a while I was lucky. I made it home in one piece every night. But good luck never goes on forever. It was only six weeks later that I got what was coming to me. Trouble is, Jim got it too.

"Do you know the place where Amherst Road bends around the bay, the place where the railway tracks run right beside the road? There's a level crossing there. People who live in Bay View, people like Jim, have to turn across the tracks there to get home. There's hardly any room between the road and the tracks there for a car to wait while the barrier is down. The rear bumpers of the waiting cars point right at the westbound traffic. Anything

much bigger than a Volkswagen Beetle almost sticks out into the oncoming traffic. You get the picture?

Well, the barrier was down, a big freight, three locomotives they tell me, was coming along. Jim was sitting there, waiting. Who could miss his red Trans Am?

"I didn't."

(Pause; drop the head; look up. Go)

"I hit him from behind with my pick-up. I was fine, hardly a bruise or a cut. Seems unfair, doesn't it? Jim? Jim went under the freight. Do you know how long it takes to stop one of those big freights? They scraped up the pieces a half mile down the track."

(Pause, a good long one this time.)

"I thought I could hold my liquor, used to boast about it in college. The strange thing was I was barely over the legal limit and I had killed a man!

"Are you sure you can hold your liquor?"

(Good. Let that one sink in. Go.)

"I guess you could say I got off pretty easy. If I'd pulled a gun on Jim I would have got a life sentence with no possibility of parole for fifteen years. As it is, they took my license and sent me to jail for three months. They let me out once a week to speak to groups like this. It's called community service, I believe. Yes, I got off easy. But I know I killed a man, and every morning I still have to look in the mirror. Every morning I still have to say to the face in the glass, 'I am a murderer.'"

(Okay; give them a minute.)

"That's about all I have to tell you this morning."

"Now you look like you're all well-brought-up young people. You look like you clap whenever a guest finishes a speech. Well, don't clap for me. I don't deserve it. Just sit there and think. Ask yourself, 'What do I want to see when I look in the mirror?' I hope you never have to see what I see every day. A murderer."

(Stop; nod silently to the principal; sit down.)

(Here comes the principal. Funny how they can never wait to get their two cents in.)

"Mr. Lang, I know that the whole school joins me in expressing our appreciation to you for your most interesting presentation. I am sure everyone will take your speech to heart. If that is the case, it may be that, while you have taken a life because of your drinking, you have perhaps saved another with your forceful message today. Perhaps that thought may offer you some comfort the next time you look in your mirror."

(Nod gravely; look thoughtful.)

"Now the senior band will favor us with a medley of tunes from Broad-way hits. Mr. Lang, you won't mind waiting till the end of the program in case some of the students would wish to speak to you?"

(Smile; wink at the bandmaster.)

"Mr. Principal, I'm in no hurry to get back to jail. I'm sure the senior band isn't that bad!"

(Good. They loved that one.)

"That they are not, Mr. Lang. Our band!"

(Good. He's down.)

Of course, I wish they could applaud. I really do deserve it, you know. Why? Because even a half-smashed forty-two-year-old can hit the rear end of a Trans Am if he wants to. And that big ol' pickup just lifted up that pain-in-the-rear partner of mine and put him exactly where I wanted him.

Of course, it took months for the right combination of circumstances to occur. I forget how many times I watched Jim sail smoothly across the tracks or passed by, tanked but frustrated, as some commuter waited in front of him.

It really was a pain drinking a pint of bourbon every day just in case that was the day. But the waiting worked out all right too. The secretary could swear on a stack of Bibles that I drove home polluted every night for months. And, of course, she did. Nothing like the truth to make a witness sound convincing.

My only real mistake was letting myself get so close to the blood alcohol limit. I had intended to be drunker than that, but when the accident happened I lost my mostly liquid lunch all over the pickup. But even that may have worked out for the best. The bourbon-smelling vomit probably had a more telling psychological effect on the police than the low breathalyzer scores.

I got about what I expected. Three months is a lot better than life in the slammer. Only two months and six more high schools to go and I'm free, free to run the company myself. And free of Jim.

What about that round of applause now?

You see, I really am a murderer.

A successful one.[1]

---

1. "I Am a Murderer," written by Stephen Farris, was first published in the *Toronto Star*, Saturday, August 10, 1985.

Red as Blood

I actually thought the story I had submitted the year before was more interesting than "I Am a Murderer." The short story as I wrote it disappeared many years ago, but here is the incident it was based on. As you will gather, this was a story that was both true and factual. It is also the kind of story that could be heard, I think, in a nonchurch setting. There is, however, a connection to things of the spirit which makes it worth telling either in or out of church.

The year before our marriage Patty lived with two friends, Pam and Lynne, in a basement apartment a few blocks north of the University of Toronto. One morning, Patty and Lynne went out together, leaving Pam to study in her room for an upcoming examination. Because Pam was in the apartment, they left the outer door unlocked. This was not unusual in Toronto in those days, but may not have been wise near the university where petty theft of student property was common. At one point, Pam said later, she thought she heard a sound in the apartment and even got up from her work to check, but no one was there.

It was probably for the best that she encountered no one, for when the others returned, they discovered that Patty had been robbed. Her jewelry had been taken, including, as she told me, a cross with a blood red stone which I had given her. She called the police, who came, took a description of the jewelry and gently admonished the girls for leaving the door unlocked, even when one of them was home. "Not safe anymore," they said.

Later that day, Patty realized that not only had she lost her jewelry, but her bedside radio was gone as were a few dollars in small bills and change. Reluctantly, she reported this further loss to the police, thinking that a telephone report on such a small matter would suffice. The police assured her, however, that an officer would come to interview her again. This was obviously a very low priority in the precinct, for it was quite some time before an officer did come to take the statement. When the officer did arrive, it was obvious that he was very young and quite possibly still a cadet. Probably the sergeant had sent him on the easiest possible duty, to interview three pleasant young women. Even by cadet standards, the officer had a very young face. Even in her early twenties Patty was learning the inevitable truth that becomes increasingly obvious as we age: the police are getting younger every year!

The officer took Patty's statement, but it was obvious that his mind was not on his work. He was quite plainly distracted and, strangely enough, when he thought no one was looking, he would sniff his tie. This happened several times until, to the young officer's embarrassment, he realized that Patty had caught him sniffing. Now, Patty is obviously a sympathetic person and the officer decided it was safe to come clean.

"Do I smell bad?" he asked.

"No, you don't," replied an astonished Patty.

"Earlier this afternoon, we got a call to one of those high-rises down on Bloor Street. The tenants were complaining about a dreadful smell from one of the apartments, and no one would answer the door. The building super called us and when we arrived; he used the master key to let us in. There was a body of a man. He had obviously died of a hemorrhage, and blood was everywhere. The corpse had been there a long time, and the smell was revolting. When we were done with the apartment, the sergeant let me go home to change out of my uniform. I changed everything, except my tie. But I can still smell the odor in the tie."

And he sniffed his tie yet again. Patty looked sympathetic, as she truly was.

"But this is the strange thing. The doctor said it took a long time for the man to die. He must have been in great pain and he was conscious, but he never called for help."

"How strange! Why not?" asked Patty.

"The walls of the apartment were lined with televisions, electronic gear, furs, you name it. We think he was a thief or a fence, and he didn't dare ask for help. People would have found out what he was."

12

Just Memories

As I have mentioned, there was a time when personal stories in the pulpit were considered less than homiletical good form. That did not stop preachers from telling such stories, of course, but they did often introduce these anecdotes with words such as, "If you will forgive a personal story, . . ." These memories are in the end nothing more than a series of personal stories, largely about marriage and family life. Perhaps you will forgive me for them. But, to be truthful, stories like these can be very useful if we end up preaching or teaching about such matters.

The Proceeds of Crime

As a bachelor, I drove a much-loved, butter-yellow 1971 MGB roadster (British for convertible) with a removable hardtop. As my wedding day approached, I was almost broke and would not earn a paycheck until I took up a summer job after the honeymoon. The honeymoon itself would be cheap, a week in a family cottage on a lake in northern Ontario, but we still had to eat for the week and pay for a hotel for the first night in Toronto. With reluctance, I was going to ask my father to loan me the money. He would have lent the money gladly, but as a matter of pride I certainly did not want to have to take advantage of his generosity. At about that time, I went to the parking lot at the seminary and found a topless roadster; somebody had removed the removable hardtop on a permanent basis. I received $225 from insurance for the hardtop, put on the soft top, and paid for the honeymoon with the insurance money. In other words, we got married on the proceeds of crime.

No, I had nothing to do with the theft and neither did Patty, my fiancée. But sometimes crime does pay!

Four Bare Legs in a Bed

That was the beginning of a happy marriage that now stands at more than forty years and counting, despite the fact that we married at what in retrospect seems a very young age. When our son and his fiancée announced their engagement, our first reaction was to say to one another, "They're too young!" Or so it seemed until we realized that they would both be older than we were when we married. Moreover, in those times long past, we did not have the benefit of formal marriage counseling. Well, in a way we received some memorable counseling.

The closest thing to marriage counseling we received was from the waitress at a deli we frequented. (The waitress loved serving me because I always "ate up," so she always arranged for me to receive larger than standard portions.) When she found out we were about to be married, she wagged her finger knowingly at the two of us, "Remember," she said, "Marriage is more than four bare legs in a bed!"

Very true! . . . Years later, when the two boys came along, we realized that marriage is actually eight bare legs in a bed.

Never Go to Bed Angry

We also received excellent advice at our wedding. We had invited Patty's honorary Uncle Bob to give thanks at the wedding banquet. Uncle Bob had been my father-in-law's best man. In the run-up to the festivities, he met my future mother-in-law's maid of honor, who, a year or so later, became Aunty Peg, as it turned out. A marriage is about connections, just as much as it is about four bare legs in a bed.

Uncle Bob read to us from Dietrich Bonhoeffer's prison letter written on the occasion of his sister's marriage. Bonhoeffer reminded the newly married couple of the scriptural injunction from Ephesians: "Do not let the sun go down on your anger," and, he continued, "but forgive one another every day

from the bottom of your heart." Uncle Bob translated this as "Never go to
bed angry with one another."

We have followed his advice and have never gone to bed angry with one
another. Mind you, we have had some very late nights.

I know which one of us has to exercise the gift of forgiveness more
often, however. Not too long ago, a friend from an internet board on
which I participate, a man whom I had never met except in e-form,
visited our city. He was born and raised in Alabama and therefore, by
birthright, a college football fan. "Roll, Tide, roll!"

After getting to know Patty a bit, he turned to me and said, "There's
an old southern saying about men with wives like yours. 'Man, you sure
outkicked your coverage.' It applies in your case."

Agreed.

Give Us the Counterpoint

Another thought has helped us in marriage. Both of us have enjoyed over
the years the detective novels of Dorothy Sayers. Dorothy Sayers was a great
scholar; her translation of Dante's Divine Comedy *has been for many years*
a standard English version of that great classic. She was also a devout Chris-
tian and a prolific author on matters spiritual, writing, for example, the
radio play, The Man Born to Be King, *which is still sometimes aired at the*
Christmas season. She is best known for her detective novels, however. These
are set in the '20s and '30s. Sayers' sleuth, Lord Peter Wimsey, falls deeply
in love with Harriet Vane, a woman detective novelist whom he has saved
from the gallows. He is, however, unsuccessful in his courtship, though not in
his criminal investigations, through the length of almost four entire novels.
Harriet fears that her individuality will be lost in a conventional marriage
to so dynamic a personality as Lord Peter. In a society of male domination,
equality would not be possible with a person of his wealth and class, with
a person to whom she owed her life. Toward the end of the fourth of those
novels, Lord Peter takes Harriet to a concert in an Oxford college where they
listen to Bach's haunting Concerto in D Minor for two violins"

As they are listening, Harriet is caught up in thoughts of Peter:

> *Peter, she felt sure, could hear the whole intricate pattern, every*
> *part separately and simultaneously, each independent and equal,*

separate but inseparable, moving over and under and through, rav-
ishing heart and mind together.

She waited till the last movement had ended and packed hall was
relaxing its attention in applause.

'Peter—what did you mean when you said that anybody could have
the harmony if they would leave us the counterpoint?

'Why,' said he, shaking his head, 'that I like my music polyphonic.
If you think I meant anything else, you know what I meant.'[1]

Harriet does know what he meant. He meant the kind of marriage they
needed was more like counterpoint than harmony. Rather than characterized
by one dominant melody, the other filling in beneath or above, their mar-
riage would be two intertwining melodies, both lovely. We too have tried for
counterpoint rather than harmony in our marriage. From time to time, on
one of the now rare occasions when I am called upon to marry a couple, I
have played the second movement of that lovely piece of music in the hope
that they too will seek the counterpoint.

Now, none of this should suggest that our marriage is idyllic. For example, I forget things. In a fit of exasperation over one particularly egregious
example of forgetfulness, Patty once announced that if I got Alzheimer's,
nobody would be able to tell. But here is one story I have managed to
remember.

The Christmas Gift

Just before Christmas one year, some friends dropped by our home while
Patty was out. I welcomed them, brewed the inevitable tea, and offered them
Christmas cake. Then, to my great discomfort, they gave us a lovely Christ-
mas card and a present. What does it say about us that there is nothing
worse at Christmas than to receive a gift and have nothing to give back?
I excused myself, looked around desperately and saw an object that looked
new. I picked it up, handed it to the guests and said, "This is what we would
like to give you for Christmas. My apologies, we haven't had the chance to
wrap it yet." The guests received the gift, though with a rather strange look
on their faces, and shortly thereafter took their leave. I felt modestly proud
of my ready thinking.

1. Sayers, *Gaudy Night.*

That is, I felt proud until Patty came home. I told her who had visited,
what I had done and identified the object I had given away.

"Stephen," Patty exclaimed. "That's what they gave us last Christmas."

But, whatever the trouble, we forgive one another before we sleep.

The Judo Throw

For many years a much-loved weekly program aired on the Canadian
Broadcasting Corporation called *The Vinyl Café*, the host of which was
Stuart McLean. The main feature of the show was a weekly story told by
McLean himself (always worth listening to). but there was also a segment
called Story Exchange. These stories were sent in by listeners, cast in the
form of a letter to Stuart himself. Of the thousands of letters sent in, one
a week was read aloud on the program. This is the one I sent in. It was
never selected. When you read it, you may wonder how I actually managed ever to get married.

Dear Stuart,

They asked me for an embarrassing high school memory—one of those "get
to-know-the-faculty in a more personal way at the start of the year sort of
things." I have no shortage of such memories in my life but here, quite liter-
ally, is—well, here's the story.

Back in the '60s my high school, an all-boys school, by the way, bought
a computer for teaching purposes. That doesn't sound like much now, but
in the '60s it was a big thing. Soon all the geeks in the school were walking
around with great piles of the IBM punch cards that were necessary in those
days for programming. Peter, one of those geeks (I think he is a multimil-
lionaire now), wrote a program to arrange blind dates. We sent forms to
all the girls' schools in the area and, sure enough, a small avalanche of
filled-out forms came back. Peter entered the information into the computer
and, whirrr, whizzz, hmmm, out came a printout with the matches. I had the
names and phone numbers of, I think, six girls, which was about six better
than I was doing without technological aid. A "Computer Dance" was set
up and those without steady girlfriends phoned their computer matches. In
a boys'' school, believe me, most of us fell into that category. I phoned the
first girl on my list, and somewhat to my surprise (some painful experiences
there) she accepted immediately.

Now, it is relevant to the story to know that I was a tackle on the football team and the center on the basketball team and generously sized even for those positions. When I arrived at her door to pick her up, I realized immediately one of the ways that the computer picked matches; it was size. She was a big girl—not fat, just big and, in memory, actually rather sweet. I was considerably better at sports than small talk and, in retrospect, I realize that she might have been suffering from similar social deficiencies. (Possibly girls in girls' schools face the same challenges as boys in boys' school. And maybe big girls can be just as awkward as big boys . . . who knows?) . . . But we did our best. As we were dancing, she let me know that in her school they were teaching judo in a self defense course. I replied, "Well, that might be all right if some little guy attacked you but what if it were a big guy like, say . . . me?" (A little cocky there, perhaps?)

She said, "Put your hand on my shoulder."

I did just that. When she tried a move, I simply pressed down hard and she couldn't do whatever it was she had planned.

Self-satisfied smile . . .

Suddenly, she changed her move. I was leaning forward, pressing down, off balance, overconfident. She turned, took my arm in both hands, rotated her hips, and tossed me over her shoulder in a full, Bruce Lee movie-style, judo throw. The next thing I knew, I was flat on my back on the dance floor looking up at my date who still had my wrist in both hands, not to mention a shocked look on her face. And all around in a huge circle my teammates and friends were staring down at me.

It was the hit of the dance.

At least she didn't put her foot on my chest.

But I still didn't try to kiss her goodnight.

Now that's the end of the story. With the vantage point of years, I now think she was probably just as embarrassed as I was. Despite this story, I actually was a fairly decent teenage boy—not the kind of boy a rather sweet girl would actually enjoy humiliating—and what happened could hardly have been her expectation for the evening either. I ought to have asked her out again or at least phoned her to tell her that nothing worse than my pride had been hurt. I never did. But then perhaps that would have required a graciousness that can hardly be expected from a seventeen-year-old boy, or at least from the boy that I was so many years ago. Still, wherever she is, I hope that if faced by a similar question about an embarrassing high school memory, she can tell her side of this story and laugh also.

And if by chance she hears this story, tell her I'm fine, and I hope she is too.

A Traditional Marriage Ceremony

Most of the stories in this book are my own, but this is a favorite that was passed on to me by my friend Joey Jeter, who formerly taught homiletics at Texas Christian University.

There once was a young couple in a small Texas town, so Joey told me, who started dating in junior high school. They kept dating through high school, and remained a couple when both went off to university. After graduation, they decided it was time to get married. There was one difficulty, however. In the meantime both their families had moved away from the town in which the young people had grown up, and they had no emotional attachment to the parents' new homes. They made the obvious decision to have the ceremony in their old hometown.

They approached the minister of the church in which they had been raised. "Pastor," they said, "Even though we are no longer members of the church and don't even live in town, would it be possible to married in the church and have you officiate at the ceremony?"

"Certainly," replied the minister. "I would be right pleased and proud to marry y'all."

"Wonderful!" they enthused. "There is one problem, however. We can't be in town until just before the wedding, so it will be difficult to plan the ceremony with you."

"No problem at all. All you have to do is tell me whether you want a contemporary wedding service or a traditional service, and I can plan the entire ceremony for you."

Very reassuring! The young couple talked it over and decided this was an excellent plan. After some further discussion, they declared they were very progressive people and they would prefer a contemporary ceremony.

"That's fine," replied their former pastor. "I can take care of all the rest."

The day of the wedding there was an enormous rainstorm, just short of a typhoon, and much of that part of Texas was underwater. That included the parking lot of the church, which had, unfortunately, become a small lake.

The last guest to arrive, the bride's Great Aunt Lucy, tried to drive her old Lincoln Town Car into the lake and stalled her car in the midst of the water. She was in obvious distress. Very gallantly, the best man took off his shoes and socks, rolled up his formal trousers past the knee and waded out to the car. He extricated Aunt Lucy from the stalled vehicle and carried her to the church door. All was well.

The best man then toweled off his legs, put on his socks and shoes and took his place with the groom's party at the front of the church. Unfortunately, he had neglected to roll down one of his trouser legs properly.

The minister caught sight of this, could imagine how everybody would feel if all the wedding photos displayed a little too much groomsman's calf, and whispered in the general direction of the groom's side of the church. "Pull down your pants!"

Now, the minister's whisper carried beyond its intended audience and everyone was shocked. The best man was shocked into immobility and did nothing.

Growing irritated by the young man's inaction, the minister repeated himself more vigorously: "I said, pull down your pants."

And the groom said, "On second thought, we'll have the traditional service!"

Our rather traditional wedding ceremony had no such catastrophes. Our fathers, both ministers, presided at the ceremony. Both have since died and listening to their voices on the cassette tape of the ceremony remains a joy. Then, of course, the children came along.

But Tomorrow I'll Stay Home . . .

Loving the Lord our God with all our heart and mind and strength means putting God first, even ahead of family, but it doesn't mean putting church and church business first. That is a distinction my sons taught me when they were little.

I remember a time early in my first ministry when I allowed myself to get too occupied with church business. I think it was when my sons, Allan and Daniel, were three years and one year old respectively. Things were going well in the church. The congregation was growing so there were meetings to attend, classes to teach and time necessary to prepare for worship.

I didn't realize just how busy I had allowed myself to become until I took
a short break. That morning, as I remember it, I was sitting on the sofa while
the boys played at my feet. Three-year-old Allan picked up a book, showed it
to me, and said, "I'm Daddy. This is my Bible."

"How cute," I thought. "He's imitating me!"

"I'm going to a meeting!" Allan announced.

Accurate, maybe, but not nearly so cute.

Allan put down his book, looked me in the eye, and said, "But maybe
tomorrow I'll stay home with my boys."

I felt as if I had been suddenly stabbed through the heart. I got up from
the sofa, found my appointment book, and drew lines through many of the
events. The church did fine without my presence at every single event, and as
far as I can tell, it was much better for the boys . . . and for me. By the way,
Patty swears she didn't put Allan up to it.

I tell that story to my students when the time comes to talk about good
time management for clergy.

Tell Me a Jesus Story, Daddy

A few years later, our family moved to Toronto where I had become a
professor of homiletics. (Here's another aside: When I left the church of
which I was minister, the church treasurer handed me the separation papers, which government regulations mandated at the end of a period of
employment. Under the space labelled, "Reason for severance of employment" the treasurer had filled in, "Left for a better job." I felt stabbed in
the heart yet again. There is no better job than being a parish minister.)

For the father of a young family, becoming a theology professor did
have the advantage of requiring fewer evening meetings and little pastoral visiting. I was now far more likely to be home in the evenings. The real
question was what I would do with those evenings.

Just about that time, a friend from graduate school days, a white South Afri-
can Anglican priest and professor of New Testament, came to visit us. Those
were still the days of apartheid, and as the evening drew on, our conversation
turned to the political situation in his homeland. Our guest mentioned that
he had been arrested during an anti-apartheid demonstration, and that he
was anxious lest he be arrested again at some point. Someday, he feared, he

might be picked up by the police without warning and would simply not come home for dinner.

Our friend had children more or less the same age as our own boys. I thought how terrible that would be for the family. "How do you handle that?" I asked. "Do you try to prepare your children for what might happen?"

He replied, "I do the one thing I can do. Every evening I am home with them, I tell them a 'Jesus story' from the Bible. 'Tell us a Jesus story,' the children say. I figure that is the only thing I have to give them that the authorities can never take away."

Once again, I felt accused. Though I had certainly often read to my sons, I had never made telling them, not reading but telling, a "Jesus story" a primary part of their lives or mine. So, over the next couple years, every evening I was home, I claimed into the lower bunk with the boys and I told them a Jesus story, starting from Genesis and working through to the end of the Bible. I did not use one of the many sanitized versions of the Bible that were available for children. I told them the stories, including the grim and violent ones, in my own words. And they listened.

Why not? They were almost stereotypical little boys, after all. We had followed standard progressive childrearing practices of the time, not allowing them to play with toy guns and giving them baby dolls to develop their nurturing side. The boys tore the arms off the dolls and used them as guns, pointing at each other the limbs bent at the elbows in shapes vaguely reminiscent of pistols and shouting, "Bang, Bang!" I would have been surprised if violent stories had upset them. But these violent stories were told in the context of the love, which is the main theme of the Bible as a whole, and by a father who, despite all his faults, loved them very dearly . . . which they knew. So of course they were ready to hear! As an aside, nothing in those stories was more violent than what was happening in, say, South Africa at that very time. Perhaps not editing out the violence helped prepare the boys to live in a world where God's love must surely work its way even through violence.

The Secret in the Story

It would be less than truthful, however, to leave you with the impression that I never told stories or read to my sons until the visit of our South African friend. For example, when Allan was, I think, about six years old and beginning to read himself, I undertook to read to him chapter by chapter, night by night, C. S. Lewis's classic, The Lion, the Witch and the Wardrobe. Daniel, two years younger and the more physically active of the boys, would play about at my feet, only occasionally listening to the story, or so I thought.

Before I began reading the book, I told the boys, "There is a secret in this story. I'm not going to tell you what it is. You'll have to figure it out for yourselves. But don't worry about the secret. It's a wonderful story, and you can enjoy it even if you do not know the secret." Allan nodded and Daniel kept playing.

Months later, when we had nearly worked our way through the story, we were all together as a family in our car. We drove past a Roman Catholic church with a very large cross at its door. Daniel looked at me and said, "Daddy, is that the cross that Jesus died on?"

"No, Daniel," I replied. "Jesus died on a cross long ago, far away, outside the city of Jerusalem. But we still put crosses on our churches to remind us that he died for us."

"Oh," said Daniel, and he grew quiet, obviously thinking about my answer. Finally, he spoke again.

"Daddy," he said. "Aslan's a lot like Jesus, isn't he?!"

"That's right!" I exclaimed. "And that's the secret in the story."

"Oh, I knew that!" said Allan scornfully.

We never quite know what children, even quite young children, will get from stories. But it will often be more than we expect. And here's another thing: when it comes to reading the Bible, as an adult and an interpreter of Scripture, I have always thought it right to read the Bible as a whole as if Jesus is the secret in the story. But whether or not this is the case, it is certain that one of the most blessed of all roles of storytelling lies in shaping our children.

The All-Nighter

I wasn't the only one in the family to tell stories, of course. My father had died before the boys were born, but the boys were deeply loved by their three remaining grandparents, and loved them right back. The boys could tell you many stories about their grandparents and the rest of the extended family, but few of these stories would be of interest beyond the family circle. There is one story, told by their grandfather, which touches on the wider world of theology, however.

My late father-in-law, Peter Gordon White, himself a fine storyteller and conversationalist, spent a year as a visiting student at Union Theological Seminary in New York, in the period immediately after World War II. Those were golden years for the seminary, and, it is said, even for the city of New York itself. The young Peter loved his year in the city that never sleeps and spoke of his time there with great fondness for the remainder of his long and productive life.

He used to tell of a time when an essay was due. He was a little behind his schedule, and the night before the paper was due he was forced to imitate the city and do without sleep. Thanks to his all-nighter, however, he managed to finish the essay, type it up, and slip it through the mail slot in his professor's office door.

By that time, it was far too late even to think of going to bed, so Peter decided to go directly to the classroom where his first lecture of the new day would take place. As it happened, that first class was with the great Reinhold Niebuhr, America's most notable theologian. At the back of the classroom was a comfortable sofa on which Peter took a seat. That may have been a mistake.

The next thing Peter knew, he was being prodded into wakefulness by someone poking him in the ribs. He opened his eyes, and there was Reinhold Niebuhr looming over him.

"Young man," said Niebuhr. "At least you could have the courtesy to wait until I begin lecturing before falling asleep!"

Conclusion

Who Are These People?

Good storytellers—whether preachers, teachers, or anything else—need to know their audience. It is hard to tell stories to people whom you do not know. I have had occasion to speak to an audience about whom I know almost nothing, as many of us have done. I adapt to the situation in my preparation and during the actual speaking by assuming that this particular congregation or audience is similar to groups I have addressed in the past. It often works, as far as I can tell, but it is always slightly uncomfortable. It is far better to have some sense of the nature of the people to whom we are speaking. This includes in obvious matters such as age, socioeconomic background, and gender distribution. (Older, middle-class, and heavily female is often the answer in the churches I speak in.) It is far more important, however, to come to a sense of who these people are theologically. Who are they, as before God? It is to them in this capacity that we speak. Here are three related ways of thinking about the people to whom we speak.

Saints

We could define our audience by its problems: it is aging, failing to reach out to those around, insufficiently committed to justice—and guilty of a number of other sins and omissions. Those sins and omissions are probably numerous. It would be easy to add here a chapter of stories of trouble in the church. Perhaps we could call it "Behaving Badly in Church." It would be a lengthy chapter and not a very pleasant read. The chapter could contain material going back to the troubled and troublesome church in Corinth to whom Paul wrote. Even a cursory reading would show that they were a collection of drunks, sex fiends, and argumentative troublemakers. Paul deals with all that in his letters, but it is not where he begins, because that is not who they truly are. He reminds them who they are right at the beginning of the letter: "To the church of God that is in Corinth, to those who are sanctified in Christ Jesus, called to be saints, together with all those who in every place call on the name of our Lord Jesus Christ, both their Lord and ours" (1 Cor 1:2).

Paul says that the main things about the Corinthians are that they are the "church of God," in that particular locality. The Greek word for "church," *ekklesia,* comes from the words to "call out." A church is the fellowship of those called out by God. Moreover, this is so because they are in a relationship collectively with Jesus Christ, in whom they are "sanctified." (I do not mean to demean the importance of a "personal relationship with Jesus Christ," but here Paul seems to be talking about "a collective relationship with Jesus Christ.") In response to God's call on them, they in turn "call on the name of the Lord Jesus Christ," and he is both their Lord and ours. And finally, and perhaps most surprisingly, Paul names them saints. Do not misunderstand the English translation, "called to be saints," as meaning that the Corinthians need to heed that call and work hard, get right with God, and become saints sometime in the future. There is, in fact, no form of the verb "to be" in the original Greek. They have been sanctified, made holy in God's eyes already. They are, more literally, the "called saints," not in some future they may achieve if they work very hard at it, but now, flawed as they are.[1] The call makes the saint.

Saint Maximilian Kolbe

This is another story I was told during my time in Eastern Europe.

During the Second World War more than Jews were sent to the Nazi con-centration camps. In those dreadful camps were gypsies, homosexuals, Poles, Communists, socialists, union leaders, Protestants, Catholics, and people who had simply been in the wrong place at the wrong time. One such person was a Polish Roman Catholic priest named Maximilian Kolbe, who was held

---

1. The structure of the passage makes description of the Corinthians as the "called saints" parallel to Paul's description of himself as a "called apostle." Paul is already an apostle. We know from Galatians how strongly Paul would react to any idea that he was not an apostle already. The call makes the apostle; the call makes the saint.

as a prisoner at Auschwitz. He was an ordinary priest and probably quite flawed in many ways, just as we are. Ironically, he himself may have been deeply anti-Semitic. But that is not the point of the story, for there is no such thing as a saint without flaws. The Nazi guards became displeased with the prisoners in Maximilian Kolbe's hut for some reason and announced that they would deliberately starve to death one out of ten prisoners, their names to be drawn by lot. Maximilian Kolbe drew one of the long straws and was safe, but standing next to him was a young Polish man—a husband, the father of young children. The young man drew a short straw but he was saved when Kolbe volunteered to take the young man's place and was executed.

Some years ago Pope John Paul II returned to his native Poland to declare Maximilian Kolbe a saint of the Roman Catholic Church. How wonderful to have a Polish pope presiding at the canonization of a Polish saint! But the pope was not the most special guest at the ceremony. There was an even more special guest at the magnificent ceremony in Kolbe's honor—an old Polish man, now a grandfather.

Of course he was there!

After all, wouldn't you be there? Wouldn't you be present at a ceremony in honor of someone who died for you?

Every time you go to church and share the bread and wine, you are.

Only, at this ceremony, you are the saint. Because, in truth, in order to become a saint, you don't have to die for somebody else. Somebody else has to die for you.

And he has.

Tell your stories to people who are saints.

God's Favorite Child

There used to be, and in some places doubtless still are, church pages in the Saturday newspaper. The page was made up largely of advertisements giving the times of worship services, the names of the preachers, and very often the titles of the sermons. Every First Steeple-type church supplied such an ad, and also a great number of churches who merely wanted to belong to that category. I always hated having to supply a sermon title. It had to be into the paper's advertising office well before I knew what I was preaching about. On those very rare occasions when I actually came up with a good title, it was almost invariably the last thing in the sermon process. Much too late for the newspaper!

Still, the results could be entertaining from time to time. There was, for example, the church in Toronto that still retained both a morning and an evening service, and whose pulpit was filled by a famously long-winded preacher, named, shall we say, the Reverend Dr. Hamish MacSporran. One weekend their advertisement let us know that the sermon would be "A Warning to All Christians!" Immediately underneath was the notice, "Dr. MacSporran will preach at both services." Kind of them to let us know!

At about the same period my brother Michael was the associate minister at a genuine first steeple church in our home city of Toronto. I was living elsewhere at the time, and Michael mailed me a clipping of the church ad that appeared one weekend when he was scheduled to preach. The sermon title was "God's Favorite Son" and underneath, "Dr. Michael Farris." And Michael had added a handwritten note, "See, Dad always did like me best!"

Maybe there is something important about that little exchange. Tell them, those people in the church, tell them stories as if you are speaking to God's favorite child, the one God likes best. For that is the way it truly is.

Christ's Brothers and Sisters

Ian Victor, a minister of my own vintage, one whom I had known off and on through the years, died suddenly and prematurely not too long ago. Ian would have been fascinated by this project, for he himself was a marvellous storyteller. He was also one of the wittiest and funniest men I have ever known, alive to the twists, turns, and humorous possibilities of language, but also a man of deep faith and commitment. (Deep faith and piercing wit is a combination that appears more often than one might think.) We do not normally use the word enjoy in connection with a funeral, but Ian's funeral was a case where the word does apply. I enjoyed being able to attend the funeral.

Ian's wife, Cathy, had invited Glenn Inglis, a longtime friend, to preach on the occasion, a rather difficult task for many reasons. I knew Glenn would do an excellent job, however, because I had heard him preach many times. He had, in fact, been my minister in Vancouver. Glenn ended his marvelous sermon by telling that when he and Ian had been neighboring ministers, they had both taken part in a study group working through the great work on the atonement by the Swedish Lutheran bishop Gustav Aulen. The book is titled Christus Victor. Ian Victor, it seemed, turned to Glenn and whispered, "He's my brother."

Glenn paused and ended the sermon with the simple words, "And so he is."

So he is for them all. The people out there are Christ's brothers and sisters. And if they don't know that already, that is what they can become. Speak, and tell stories as if you believe it.

Bibliography

Alter, Robert. *The Art of Biblical Narrative*. New York: Basic Books, 2011.

Boone, Dan. *Preaching the Story That Shapes Us*. Kansas City: Beacon Hill, 2008.

Brewer, James. "A Dutch Admiral Who Rescued from the Galleys Men Persecuted for Their Faith . . ." http://www.allaboutshipping.co.uk/2015/09/27/a-dutch-admiral-who-rescued-from-the-galleys-men-persecuted-for-their-faith/.

Burghardt, Walter. *Preaching: The Art and the Craft*. New York: Paulist, 1987.

Buttrick, David. *Homiletic: Moves and Structures*. Philadelphia: Fortress, 1987.

Casas, Bartolomé de las. *A Short Account of the Destruction of the Indies*. Edited by Anthony Pagden. Translated by Nigel Griffin. London: Penguin Classics, 1992.

Corbett, Edward P. J., and Robert J. Connors. *Classical Rhetoric for the Modern Student*. 4th ed. New York: Oxford University Press, 1998.

Cothen, Joe. *The Old, Old Story: A Guide for Narrative Preaching*. Gretna, LA: Pelican, 2003.

Craddock, Fred. *Craddock Stories*. Edited by Michael Graves and Richard F. Ward. St. Louis: Chalice, 2001.

———. "When the Roll Is Called Down Here." http://www.youtube.com/watch?v=X2oSd8NKLsk/.

———. "When the Roll Is Called Down Here." http://www.preachingtoday.com/sermons/sermons/2010/july/whentherolliscalleddownhere.html/.

Cron, Lisa. *Wired for Story: The Writer's Guide to Using Brain Science to Hook Readers from the Very First Sentence*. New York: Ten Speed, 2012.

Dodd, C. H. *The Parables of the Kingdom*. New York: Scribner, 1961.

Ellingsen, Mark. *The Integrity of Biblical Narrative: Story in Theology and Proclamation*. 1990. Reprint, Eugene, OR: Wipf & Stock, 2002.

Eliot, T. S. *Murder in the Cathedral*. London: Faber & Faber, 1968.

Eslinger, Richard. *Narrative & Imagination: Preaching the Worlds that Shape Us*. Minneapolis: Fortress, 1995.

———. *A New Hearing: Living Options in Homiletic Method*. Nashville: Abingdon, 1987.

———. *The Web of Preaching: New Options in Homiletic Method*. Nashville: Abingdon, 2002.

Farris, Stephen. *Grace: A Preaching Commentary*. Nashville: Abingdon, 2003.

———. "I Am a Murderer." *Toronto Star*, August 10, 1985.

———. "John Calvin and the Preaching of the Lively Word." In *Calvin@500: Theology, History and Practice* edited by Richard R. Topping and John A. Vissers, 113–27. Eugene, OR: Wipf & Stock, 2011.

————. *Preaching That Matters: The Bible and Our Lives*. Louisville: Westminster John Knox, 1998.

Fitzpatrick, Megan. "Missouri Mom Plotted Kidnapping of Her 6-Year-Old to Scare Him, Police Say." http://www.cbc.ca/news/world/missouri-mom-plotted-kidnapping-of-her-6-year-old-to-scare-him-police-1.2947534/.

Frei, Hans. *The Eclipse of Biblical Narrative: A Study in Eighteenth and Nineteenth Century Hermeneutics*. New Haven: Yale University Press, 1980.

Gottschall, Jonathan. *The Storytelling Animal: How Stories Make Us Human*. Boston: Mariner, 2013.

Green, Garrett, ed. *Scriptural Authority and Narrative Imagination*. 1987. Reprint, Eugene, OR: Wipf & Stock, 2000.

Hoezee, Scott. *Actuality: Real Life Stories for Sermons That Matter*. Artistry of Preaching Series 2. Nashville: Abingdon, 2014.

Hogan, Lucy Lind. "Rethinking Persuasion: Developing an Incarnational Theology of Preaching." *Homiletic* 24/2 (1999) 1–12.

Jacks, G. Robert. *Just Say the Word: Writing for the Ear*. Grand Rapids: Eerdmans, 1996.

John Paul, II, Pope. "Address of His Holiness John Paul II at the Ecumenical Meeting with the Protestant and Orthodox Hungarian Communities." Calvinist Church of Debrecen. Sunday, August 18, 1991. https://w2.vatican.va/content/john-paul-ii/en/speeches/1991/august/documents/hf_jp-ii_spe_19910818_celebraz-ecum-debrecen.html/.

Karia, Akash. *Public Speaking: Storytelling Techniques for Electrifying Presentations*. Self-published, AkashKaria.com/, 2014.

————. *TED Talks Storytelling: 23 Storytelling Techniques from the Best TED Talks*. Self-Published, CreateSpace, 2015.

Kelly, Benjamin. *Preaching to Connect Truth to Life: The Power of Narrative to Tell the Story*. Indianapolis: Wesleyan, 2012.

Kelsey, David H. *The Uses of Scripture in Recent Theology*. Philadelphia: Fortress, 1975.

King, Thomas. *The Truth about Stories: A Native Narrative*. Massey Lectures Series. Toronto: House of Anansi, 2003.

Lischer, Richard. *The Company of Preachers: Wisdom on Preaching, Augustine to the Present*. Grand Rapids: Eerdmans, 2002.

————. "Why I Am Not Persuasive." *Homiletic* 24/2 (1999) 13–16.

Lowry, Eugene L. *Doing Time in the Pulpit: The Relationship between Narrative and Preaching*. Nashville: Abingdon, 1985.

Lundblad, Barbara K. *Marking Time: Preaching Biblical Stories in Present Tense*. Nashville: Abingdon, 2007.

Moore, James W. *Daddy, Is That Story True, or Were You Just Preaching?* Nashville: Abingdon, 2012.

Moore, Stephen D. *Literary Criticism and the Gospels: The Theoretical Challenge*. New Haven: Yale University Press, 1989.

Olson, Roger E. *The Mosaic of Christian Belief: Twenty Centuries of Unity and Diversity*. 2nd ed. Downers Grove, IL: IVP Academic, 2016

Parker, T. H. L. *Calvin's Preaching*. Edinburgh: T. & T. Clark, 1992.

Powell, Mark. *What Is Narrative Criticism?* Guides to Biblical Scholarship: New Testament Series. Minneapolis: Fortress, 1990.

Reid, Robert et al. "Preaching as the Creation of an Experience: The Not-So-Rational Revolution of the New Homiletic." *Journal of Communication and Religion* 12 (1995) 1–9.

Rice, Charles L. *The Embodied Word: Preaching as Art and Liturgy*. Fortress Resources for Preaching. Minneapolis: Fortress, 1991.

Sachs, Jonah. *Winning the Story Wars: Why Those Who Tell—and Live—the Best Stories Will Rule the Future*. Cambridge: Harvard Business Review Press, 2012.

Salter, Darius. *Preaching as Art: Biblical Storytelling for a Media Generation*. Kansas City: Beacon Hill, 2008.

Sayers, Dorothy L. *Gaudy Night*. Kindle ed. Mustbe Interactive, 2014

Simmons, Annette. *The Story Factor: Inspiration, Influence, and Persuasion through the Art of Storytelling*. New York: Basic Books, 2006.

Warren, Rick. *The Purpose-Driven Life: What on Earth Am I Here For?* Grand Rapids: Zondervan, 1997.

Willimon, William H. *Conversations with Barth on Preaching*. Nashville: Abingdon, 2006.